GENNADEION MONOGRAPHS I

THE
VENETIANS IN ATHENS
1687–1688

FROM THE ISTORIA OF CRISTOFORO IVANOVICH

EDITED BY
JAMES MORTON PATON

THE GENNADEION MONOGRAPHS · III
PUBLISHED FOR THE AMERICAN SCHOOL OF CLASSICAL STUDIES AT ATHENS

HARVARD UNIVERSITY PRESS
CAMBRIDGE
1940

THE VENETIANS IN ATHENS
1687–1688

FROM THE *ISTORIA* OF CRISTOFORO IVANOVICH

EDITED BY
JAMES MORTON PATON

PUBLISHED FOR
THE AMERICAN SCHOOL OF CLASSICAL STUDIES AT ATHENS

HARVARD UNIVERSITY PRESS
CAMBRIDGE, MASSACHUSETTS
1940

COPYRIGHT 1940
BY THE PRESIDENT AND FELLOWS OF HARVARD COLLEGE
PUBLISHED 1940
ALL RIGHTS RESERVED

PRINTED IN THE UNITED STATES OF AMERICA

With this volume the American School of Classical Studies at Athens initiates a series of publications which will appear under the general title of Gennadeion Monographs. These monographs will be devoted to the publication of the rich source material in the Gennadeion Library and to general studies in related fields. It may be expected, therefore, that most volumes of the series will be concerned with various problems of Byzantine, mediaeval, and modern times. For the convenience of the reader the format has been reduced somewhat in size from that of most of the other scientific publications of the School. Succeeding volumes will appear in the same size unless some change is necessary for the proper presentation of exceptional material.

THE COMMITTEE ON PUBLICATIONS

PREFACE

This little book, which has been given the honor of opening the series of Gennadeion Monographs, does not attempt to tell the whole story of the Venetian occupation of Athens, but aims rather at shedding a little fresh light on some of its phases, first by presenting in the narrative of Ivanovich the version apparently current at the time in Venice, and then by illustrating or correcting this account, partly from the usual printed sources, but especially from unpublished and, so far as I am aware, largely unexamined manuscripts in Venice and Florence.

The manuscripts in Venice are the most important and the best known. The correspondence of Morosini, including the minutes of the Council of War, has of course been exhaustively studied by Laborde and other scholars, but such is its volume and variety that no small amount of new information may still be gleaned from it, chiefly on topics which have hitherto attracted little attention. The *Avvisi* of the Inquisitori di Stato, known to Laborde only from copies in the library of Rawdon Brown, have been briefly described by Lambros, but neither his publications nor the extracts in this volume give an adequate idea of the extremely miscellaneous, if often trifling, contents of this official newspaper.

In Florence the case is quite different. So far as I know, the volumes in the Archives of the Uffizi containing the letters sent from Venice to the Grand Duke twice a week by the resident Tuscan agents have been wholly neglected by students of this period. Yet they have preserved many incidents of life in Venice during the war, and enable us to follow almost from day to day the course of events as seen in the city itself, as well as the manifold fluctuations in popular opinion under the influence of the news—or often the absence of news—from the Levant. It is indeed to additional material derived from all these documents, official and unofficial, that the four Appendices owe their origin. They deal with subjects which receive scant notice from Ivanovich and in general only brief mention from later historians. It would seem, however, that at the time they aroused considerable interest and not a little discussion in Venice, and even now some acquaintance with them may perhaps contribute to a better appreciation of certain characteristic episodes of this war.

My very sincere and grateful thanks are due especially to the Harvard College Library for permission to publish these extracts from the manuscript of Ivanovich, and also to the Archivio di Stato, the Biblioteca Marciana, and the Biblioteca del Civico Museo Correr in Venice, to the Archivio di Stato in Florence, and to the Bibliothèque Nationale in Paris for numerous courtesies received in the course of this investigation.

JAMES M. PATON.

CONTENTS

	PAGE
Preface	vii
Abbreviations	xi
Chapter I. Cristoforo Ivanovich	3
Chapter II. The Occupation of Athens	9
Chapter III. The Abandonment of Athens	19

Appendices

I. Turenne	29
II. Mistra	32
III. The Withdrawal of the Army from Athens	37
IV. The Opposition to Morosini	47

| Notes | 57 |
| Index | 103 |

ABBREVIATIONS

Manuscripts

Arch. Med.—Florence. Archivio di Stato. Archivio Mediceo dopo il Principato.

1577: *Lettere al Segretario Apollonio Bassetti; Venezia e Dominio, 1687, 1688*. The volume contains, along with many other letters, the correspondence of Alessandro Guasconi, senior partner in the firm of Guasconi and Verrazzano, the Grand Duke's bankers in Venice, with the Abate Bassetti, confidential Segretario di Camera of Cosimo III. The folios in this manuscript are not numbered. The letters of Guasconi and the minutes of Bassetti's answers are numbered consecutively, but not the numerous enclosures.

3043 and 3044: *Venezia; Matteo del Teglia, Lettere e Minuti, 1685, 1686, 1687,* and *1688, 1689*. These two enormously thick volumes contain the letters and *Avvisi* sent by Matteo del Teglia, Maestro di Posta di Firenze, from Venice to F. Panciatichi, Primo Segretario di Stato, with minutes of the replies.

Consulta di Guerra, or Council of War.—Venice. Civico Museo Correr (Biblioteca). Archivio Morosini e Grimani, 138, II (Collocamento 428), *Consulta di Guerra, 1686, 20 Sett.-1689, 2 Sett.* All quotations from the minutes are copied from this volume, unless accompanied by a reference to Laborde.

Inquisitori.—Venice. Archivio di Stato. Inquisitori di Stato, *Avvisi di Venezia, 1687-1711*, Busta 705. For notes and brief extracts from the *Avvisi* for 1687 and 1688 see S. P. Lambros, Νέος Ἑλληνομνήμων, XVIII, 1924, pp. 268-271, and for the *Avvisi* of Nov. 1, 1687 (in part) and Nov. 8, 1687, *ibid.*, XX, 1926, pp. 209-214.

Misc. Med.—Florence. Archivio di Stato. Miscellanea Medicea, Filza 667: *Venezia; Matteo del Teglia al Abate P. A. Conti, 1687*. Letters and *Avvisi*, the latter often the same as those in Arch. Med., 3043. The Abate Paolo Antonio Conti was the secretary of Cardinal Ferdinando de' Medici, brother of Cosimo III.

Morosini, *Dispacci.*—Venice. Civico Museo Correr (Biblioteca). Mss. Correr, I, 299 (Colloc. 772), *Dispacci del Capitan Generale Francesco Morosini, 31 Maggio, 1686–19 Maggio, 1688.* Unless otherwise indicated, all quotations from the letters of Morosini are copied from this volume. The letter of October 10, 1687, is published in full by N. Varola and P. Volpato, *Dispaccio di Francesco Morosini, Capitan Generale da Mar, intorno al bombardamento e della presa d' Atene, l' anno 1687.* Venezia, 1862. (Per le Nozze Morosini-Costantini).

Muazzo.—Venice. Biblioteca Marciana. Mss. ital., VII, 172, Francesco Muazzo, *Storia della Guerra tra li Veneti e Turchi dall' anno 1684 a 1698.* There is a modern copy of this manuscript in Paris, Bibliothèque Nationale, Fonds ital., 2081.

Rel. Marc.—Venice. Biblioteca Marciana. Mss. ital., VII, 656, fols. 103-104, *Relatione dell' operato dell' armi Venete doppo la sua partenza da Corinto, e della presa d' Attene.* Published in full by S. P. Lambros, Δελτίον τῆς ἱστορικῆς καὶ ἐθνολογικῆς ἑταιρίας, V, 1896-1900, pp. 222-227. Extracts in Laborde, pp. 145-146, note.

Vitt. Eman.—Rome. Biblioteca Nazionale Vittorio Emanuele. Mss. Vitt. Eman., 755, 756, *Avvisi diversi, Luglio-Dec., 1687; Gen.-Giugno, 1688.* The *Avvisi* are from many other parts of Europe as well as Venice.

Books

Beregani. — *Historia delle Guerre d' Europa dalla comparsa dell' Armi Ottomane nell' Hungheria, l' anno 1683.* Venezia, 1698. 2 vols.

Foscarini.—*Historia della Republica Veneta.* Venetia, 1696.

Garzoni.—*Istoria della Repubblica di Venezia in tempo della Sacra Lega contro Maometto IV.* Quarta Impressione, Venezia, 1720. 2 vols. All references are to volume I.

Laborde.—*Athènes aux XVe, XVIe, et XVIIe siècles.* Paris, 1854. 2 vols. All references are to volume II.

Locatelli. — *Racconto historico della Veneta Guerra in Levante.* Colonia, 1691. Two volumes in one.

ABBREVIATIONS

Periodicals

A. J. A.—*American Journal of Archaeology.*

C. r. Acad. Insc.—*Comptes rendues de l' Académie des Inscriptions et Belles-Lettres.*

Δελτίον.—Δελτίον τῆς ἱστορικῆς καὶ ἐθνολογικῆς ἑταιρίας.

N. E.—Νέος Ἑλληνομνήμων.

R. ét. gr.—*Revue des études grecques.*

Z. bild. K.—*Zeitschrift für bildende Kunst.*

In the quotations from manuscripts I have generally modernized the often inconsistent capitalization, accentuation, and punctuation; in those from books I have followed the printed text in these particulars. I have also expanded abbreviations.

THE VENETIANS IN ATHENS
1687–1688

CHAPTER I

Cristoforo Ivanovich

On September twenty-first, 1687, the Venetian fleet and army entered the harbor of Piraeus; on September twenty-sixth an explosion caused by a Venetian bomb irretrievably ruined the Parthenon; on April eighth, 1688, Morosini sailed away from a deserted city, abandoning a conquest which had proved, as he had anticipated, of no military value, and indeed is now remembered only for the destruction of the most perfect monument of Athenian architecture.

More than eighty years ago the Comte de Laborde published the history of this worse than useless expedition, supported by a careful review of the then available evidence with abundant quotations from the dispatches of Morosini and other contemporary documents; and although later discoveries have revealed new facts and modified some of his conclusions, his narrative still remains unaltered in essentials. Nevertheless since we have recently passed the two hundred and fiftieth anniversary of one of the earliest and surely one of the most deplorable instances of "military necessity" directing modern weapons against a supreme work of art, this seems an appropriate moment for endeavoring with the aid of unpublished material to present the familiar story as it was told at the time in Venice and to point out some of the almost inevitable errors and omissions. Such a contemporary account is contained in the following extracts from a manuscript in the Harvard College Library, entitled *Istoria della Lega Ortodossa contra il Turco*, by Cristoforo Ivanovich, Canon of San Marco.[1]

Of the author little is known beyond the very fragmentary information scattered through his works.[2] He was born in

1628 at Budua in southern Dalmatia not far from Cattaro, and belonged to one of the noble families who after the Turkish conquest continued to enjoy the position of Venetian subjects.[3] His life at home, where he is said to have pursued his studies with some success, was rudely interrupted by the outbreak in 1645 of the long Cretan war between the Turks and Venice.[4] The fighting soon spread to the Turkish coast of the Adriatic, exposed as it was to the raids of the Venetian fleet, and Ivanovich, who evidently had no liking for conditions where, as he says,[5] "al lampo dell' Armi, meglio ch' al lume della Lucerna di Cleante si rischiarono gl' ingegni," finally took refuge in Italy.[6] He first spent three years in Verona, endeavoring apparently to improve his command of Tuscan [7] and to develop his facility as a writer of prose and verse in the local Academies, especially in the Filarmonica of which he was a member.[8]

In 1657 he moved to Venice [9] and became Secretary to Leonardo Pesaro, Procurator of San Marco,[10] but continued to follow, so far as possible, the life which he had led at Verona, attending diligently the Academies—he was a member and later Censor of the Delfica—and devoting his leisure to his poems, for which the vicissitudes of the war furnished ample material.[11] His verses were evidently well received, and Martinioni's *Catalogo* shows that by 1663 he had attained a recognized position among contemporary writers.[12] During the following years (1663-1674) he added to his reputation by securing the degree of J. U. D.,[13] by composing five *drammi per musica*, which are said to have been performed with considerable success not only at Venice but also at Vienna and Piacenza,[14] and by writing a long poem in three books on the heroic, though unsuccessful, defense of Candia by Francesco Morosini.[15] Up to this time he seems to have printed comparatively little except the *drammi*, but in 1675 he published his *Poesie*, which contained, in addition to his verses, his prose panegyric on Lazzaro Mocenigo and a selection from his correspondence with his friends among the *letterati*. The poems, which he described in the preface as " una scelta di quelle [poesie] con le quali ho sodisfatto più al proprio genio, che agl' impulsi autorevoli degl' Amici," [16] show no signs of any inspiration, and rarely rise above the mediocrity which, as Medin has pointed out, characterizes the verse of the time.[17] Ivanovich was clearly no poet, but then neither were most of his Venetian contemporaries, and the favor which his compositions apparently enjoyed shows that they corresponded to the taste, deplorably bad as it now seems, of the Academic circles in which he moved.

All these literary activities evidently did not interfere with the performance of his duties as Secretary; indeed they must have enhanced, if anything, the esteem in which he was held, for in 1676, when Pesaro was chosen one of the four special ambassadors sent to congratulate the new Pope, Innocent XI, on his election, he made Ivanovich his *Maestro di Camera*, and also secured for him an appointment as minor canon at San Marco.[18] It is possible that on his return from Rome he gave up his position with Pesaro, for in 1678 he was living in the Canonica Ducale.[19] Three years later he was promoted to the dignity of canon by the Doge, Luigi Contarini,[20] and very characteristically showed his gratitude for this preferment by composing in honor of his patron a Serenata, *La Felicità Regnante*, which was duly performed at the Canonica on September 4, 1681.[21]

In the same year he published the first part of his *Minerva al Tavolino*, a collection of letters and poems, to which he appended *Memorie Teatrali di Venezia*, a chronological list of the *drammi musicali* produced in Venice between 1637 and 1680, which is still of value for the history of the Venetian stage.[22] The book was evidently successful, for it was reprinted to accompany the second part, which appeared in 1688. In both these volumes the poems, chiefly sonnets and other occasional verses, occupy a minor place, but except in their brevity do not differ essentially from his earlier productions. The letters show us Ivanovich corresponding with a wide circle of friends on a variety of topics, but apart from descriptions of scenes in Venice and, for our subject, the letters to Morosini and Cornaro,[23] they contain very little that is noteworthy in style or substance. In fact the suspicion arises that in the publication of these letters, as before in the composition of his poems, he was indulging his " proprio genio," and seeking to justify and perpetuate the literary reputation which he felt that he had already established. The apologetic references to his " debole Musa " and to his ignorance of Tuscan need not be taken too seriously, and the place given in the collection to the highly laudatory recommendation of Lupis,[24] as well as to sundry congratulations on his preferments,[25] may perhaps be best explained by his own satisfaction at the evidence thus afforded of the position which he, a foreigner by birth, had gained in Venice. If we feel that his actual accomplishments hardly warrant such a position, we must bear in mind that Lupis enlarges on his amiable disposition and his readiness to remember favors but to forget injuries [26]—qualities which might well attract friends and predispose to favorable criticism.

Even before the publication of the *Minerva* he had taken steps to ensure that his name should not be forgotten, for on December 8, 1680, he had purchased for 80 ducats space for a monument on the south wall of the newly rebuilt church of San Moisè and for a tomb in the pavement in front of it. It would seem, however, that as his plans developed he found this site inadequate, and accordingly on September 24, 1684, he paid 50 ducats more for permission to exchange it for the place on the north wall where he promptly erected the existing baroque monument, the work of Marco Beltrame, but probably designed by Ivanovich himself.[27] The slab in the pavement, which was to mark his grave, is shown by its inscription to have been laid in 1684, and the whole work was certainly finished during his lifetime.[28] Otherwise his will, which makes ample provision for the annual cleaning of his monument, would hardly have failed to provide also for its completion.[29] This will, drawn up on October 30, 1688, was published on January 6, 1689, and accordingly, in the absence of more precise information, we may reasonably assume that he died late in December, 1688, or perhaps at the beginning of January, 1689.[30]

The *Istoria della Lega Ortodossa*, which had occupied the last years of his life,[31] was of course left a fragment, ending somewhat abruptly with the preparations of the Turks to prevent the advance of the imperial army against Belgrade in the spring of 1688. Yet this fragment is substantially complete for the period covered. Occasional marginal notes show Ivanovich adding or correcting details,[32] but there seem to be no large gaps left for later treatment, and we may conclude that the author regarded this part of his work as merely needing some final touches.

A critical estimate of the value of this history as a whole lies outside the scope of this monograph, and indeed would require a much more detailed study of the rest of the manuscript than I have been able to undertake. In the portion here printed we shall find Ivanovich deriving his information very largely from the *Avvisi* or Bulletins issued by the Venetian Inquisitori di Stato, while his topography and history are often taken with little change except necessary abbreviation from the publications of Coronelli. Obviously these easy-going methods could not produce a work of great importance or one likely to add much to our knowledge; on the other hand such a compilation may well present a fairly complete and accurate picture of the course of events as seen by an intelligent Venetian in the somewhat uncertain light of official statements. In the following notes I hope to show how this picture was composed and in what respects it was defective.

CHAPTER II

THE OCCUPATION OF ATHENS

[The preceding pages [1] have described Morosini's voyage around the Morea, from the Corinthian to the Saronic Gulf, his bombardment of Monemvasia, and his arrival at Corinth.]

Non mai stanca la mente guerriera del Capitan Generale d' essercitarsi nelle militari fatiche, chiamò la consulta da guerra per deliberare ciò che restava da operarsi in un mese e mezzo che ancora restava di campagna. Si decretò nella medesima di cogliere le presenti favorevoli congiunture della costernazione dell' esercito nemico, che disperso doppo la sconfitta riportata nelle campagne di Patrasso dalle nostre vittoriose armi s' attrovava ridotto in Tebe in solo numero di dieci mila uomini, di rivolgere quelle forze all' impresa della Fortezza d' Atene,[2] col riflesso, che soggiogata anco l' Acaia, oltre l' acquisto per se stesso rimarcabile a riguardo della fertilità del paese e negotio florido che manteneva quella scala, s' assicurarebbe nello stesso tempo dalle nemiche invasioni il conquistato regno della Morea, e si stabilirebbe a quei sudditi in avvenire la quieta e la pace.

Seguito dunque il giorno delli 20 Settembre l' embarco delle milizie sopra le galere e galeazze, consistente in 8 mila fanti e 600 cavalli,[3] si veleggiò tutta quella notte con prospero vento alla volta del Porto Lione,[4] dove approdato la mattina seguente seguì senza minima dilazione di tempo o contrasto de' nemici lo sbarco di tutte le milizie. [Questo Porto fu così detto da un leone di marmo di piedi dieci d' altezza ch' era posto su le rive del di lui fondo. È situato alle sponde settentrionali del Golfo d' Engia. Il di lui ingresso è alquanto stretto e di dentro è di buonissimo fondo, capace di molte vele. Di qui dicono essersi partito Menesteo per andar a Troia con le navi e prima di lui Teseo quando andò per pagar la pena a Minoe della morte d' Androgeo.][5]

Alla comparsa di quest' armata si portarono li principali Greci della città ad umiliarsi all' Eccellenza del Capitan Generale e con espressioni di tutta divozione verso il riverito di lui nome, offerirono le proprie sostanze e le vite stesse per le maggiori glorie della Republica. Furono accolti benignamente, inanimiti al fedel vassallaggio, et assicurati di paterna dilezione e di opportuna difesa contra i Turchi. Dagli stessi si rilevò essere li Turchi abili al maneggio dell' armi nella Fortezza in numero di 600 con rissoluzione costantissima di voler difendersi, lusingati dalla speranza d'essere soccorsi dal Seraschiero. A tal aviso ordinò Sua Eccellenza senza dilazione di tempo la marchia dell' essercito nel Borgo, lontano dalla marina cinque miglia in circa, situato a pie del monte della Fortezza, tanto più che i Turchi, che lo abitavano, s' erano ritirati nella medesima per timore. Esseguì prontamente il Conte Chinismark l' ordine con la marchia delle genti, assistendolo il Proveditor in Campo Dolfin, avanzando la sera di 22, lungi due miglia in circa dentro ad un bosco d' olivari.[6]

Alli 23 inviò a tutta diligenza al campo quattro cannoni da 20 e due di nuova invenzione da 50 e quattro mortari da bombe, che fu tutto condotto dalle ciurme delle galere. S' avanzò l' essercito al Borgo senza alcuno ostacolo de' nemici rinserati nella Fortezza. Vi piantò l' attaco il Generale il detto giorno,[7] e all' opportuno arrivo de' cannoni e mortari suddetti si principiò a bersagliarla, con la stessa assistenza del Capitan Generale, che si volle portar al campo per maggiore accudire a quella impresa. Dal tormento continuo de' fuochi ne risentivano gli assediati notabile detrimento a riguardo del recinto angusto della Fortezza.[8] Avvertito Sua Eccellenza trovarsi nel Tempio di Minerva le monizioni de' Turchi insieme con le loro principali donne e figli, stimandosi ivi sicuri per la grossezza delle mura e volti del detto tempio, ordinò al Conte Mutoni che dirizzasse il tiro delle sue bombe a quella parte.[9] Nacque sino dal principio qualche disordine nel getto delle medesime, che cadeano fuori, e fu per l' inegualità del peso che si trovò in 130 libre di svario dall' una all' altra; ma praticatosi il giusto peso non andò più fuori alcuna, si che una di quelle colpendo nel fianco del tempio finì di romperlo.[10] Ne seguì un effetto terribile nella gran furia di foco, polvere, e granate che ivi si trovavano, anzi lo sbaro e rimbombo delle suddette monizioni fece tremare tutte le case del Borgo, quale sembrava una gran città, e mise un gran spavento negli assediati, restando in questo modo rovinato quel famoso Tempio di Minerva, che tanti secoli e tante guerre non aveano potuto distruggere.

Mentre con vigore continuava l' assedio, scopertosi la mattina di 28 nell' alba il soccorso nemico consistente in due mila cavalli e mille fanti in quelle campagne, parve proprio alla versata esperienza del Generale Conte di Chinismark d' andarci per incontrarlo, tal essendo stata la precedente intenzione del Generalissimo in caso succedesse a comparsa de' Turchi; onde presa la cavalleria e l' infanteria oltramarina se li oppose, e a sola vista delle truppe Cristiane si diedero i Turchi ad una precipitosa fuga. In questo mentre il Proveditor di Campo Delfino (*sic*) con indifessa applicazione, coll' esporsi più volte alle moschettate per accelarare il travaglio de' cannone e delle bombe, cercò di stringere viepiù la Fortezza, e di necessitar i Turchi alla resa. Avertito il Mutoni da un Greco che in una casa erano ritirate alcune donne dell' Aga[11] diresse i tiri alla medesima e una bomba fece si fiera stragge di quelle che atterrita tutta la Fortezza, desperata anco del soccorso fuggato, convenne esporre bandiera bianca per rendersi, e fu lo stesso giorno a ore 22.

S' approssimò il Generale Chinismark alla Fortezza per intender l' intenzione de' Turchi, che era di rendersi a patto non potendo più a lungo soffrire il calore del foco che in diversi luoghi ardeva nella Fortezza. A questi il Prencipe di Turena,[12] che ivi era presente, fece dimandar per un suo schiavo se avessero avuto paura delle bombe, ed un di loro adirato rispose, se non fossero state queste, la Fortezza non si rendeva; e con ragione potè parlar in tal modo il Turco. È piantata la Fortezza sopra un grebbano, specie di durissimo sasso in grand' altezza, ed inaccessibile per tre parti, e impenetrabile a qualsivoglia mina.

Si stabilirono le capitolazioni della loro resa: di lasciare tutte le loro armi nella Fortezza; di partir con le loro donne e figli, e con quella robba, che cadauno potrà portare dalla Fortezza alla Marina in un solo viaggio; di noleggiare tre bastimenti forestieri per il loro imbarco e viaggio per Smirne.[13] Fu il tutto spedito al Capitan Generale nel Porto, *con 5 principali Turchi* da cui sotto li 30 Settembre fu sottoscritta la carta, *e trattenuti cortesemente* [essi Turchi sopra la galeazza Quirini per ostaggi sino l' effetuazione del capitolato. Volle Sua Eccellenza portarsi il primo Ottobre al campo con molti nobili, tutti a cavallo, et anco al Borgo per osservar le cose bissognate e per applicare ordini opportuni, colà trattenendosi tutto quel giorno, e la notte si restituì alla sua Generalizia].[14] Così li 3 Ottobre presero viaggio i Turchi, e la Republica il possesso di questa inespugnabile Fortezza. Uscirono in numero di circa tre mille e tra questi 600 uomini d' arme.[15] Altri trecento del corpo dello stesso presidio, inspirati dal vero lume del Cielo, vollero trattenersi per mondare l' impurità delle anime con l' acque del Santo Battesimo.

Entrò al governo e alla direzione della Città e Fortezza si considerabile, d' ordine del Capitan Generale, Daniel Dolfin Quarto, il quale nella carica accennata di Proveditore Straordinario in Campo rese dal tempo dell' attacco sino al fine prove moltiplici del suo valore, abilità ed esperienza. Si segnalò pure nel medesimo con attestati corrispondenti di coraggioso fervore l' altro Proveditore in Campo, Zorzi Benzon, con la sovraintendenza alla cavalleria. Seguirono il loro degno esempio li nobili che continuarono gli incomodi della campagna con molto merito, Nicolò Capello Secundo, Andrea Pisani, Alessandro Valier, Ferigo Marcello e Pietro Emo.[16] Immortalò l' uso ed impiego delle bombe con pieni testimonij della sua grande esperienza il Sopraintendente, Conte San Felice Mutoni.[17] Fece Sua Eccellenza entrare con presidio provisionale il Condottier di genti d' armi, Conte Tomeo Pompei, nella Fortezza; ove fu d' uopo impiegare qualche giorno per isgombrarla da molto numero de' corpi nemici estinti dal fuoco e purgarla insiemme dalle rovine. Il famoso Tempio di Minerva, distrutto e diroccato dalle bombe a causa d' abbruggiare tutti li grani ed altri apprestamenti da bocca, che in quello aveano ricovrati i nemici, era composto dal più fino marmo e sostenuto da 32 colone, già da' Turchi convertito in superbissima moschea.

Atene [18] è città antichissima della Grecia, con titolo archiepiscopale, metropoli dell' Attica; giace non lungi dalle piaggie del Golfo d' Engia, parte del mar Ionio, edificata dal Re Cecrope che Cecropia la disse. Fu accresciuta in perfezione dal Re Teseo che l'aggrandì, obligando tutti gli abitanti della campagna a popolarla. Cecropia precisamente chiamavasi la sua citadella, alla quale dopo fu dato anco il nome d' Acropolis. Questa è eretta sopra vivo sasso ovunque inaccessibile, detrattone dalla parte d' occidente ove vi è il suo ingresso. Da levante e mezzogiorno le muraglie formano la facciata d' un quadro; l' altre due, accomodandosi alla base formatagli dal medesimo sasso, non riescono del tutto regolari. Il circuito consiste in mille e doecento e più passi. Al basso della collina si scuoprono i vestigij d' alta muraglia, che girando un tempo le radici della medesima tanto più rendeano inaccessibile la salita. La situazione della città è molto vantaggiosa alla salute degli abitanti perchè essendo il clima caldo, siegue di grand utile l' esser ella esposta alla tramontana.[19]

Di questa famosissima città piene sono l' istorie, e delle sue antichità ne scrive difusamente Pausania, e vi restò in questi tempi qualche reliquia degna d' osservazione.

Il Tempio della Vittoria d' architettura Ionica, fatto da' Turchi magazino per polvere.

L'Arsenale di Licurgo d' ordine Dorico, sul quale come in deposito conservavano e custodivano l' armi gli Ottomani.

Era il Tempio di Minerva d' ordine Dorico ridotto in moschea, ma resta distrutto dalle bombe.

La Lanterna di Demostene, che serve d' ospicio a PP. Capuccini.

La Torre Octogona de' Veneti (sic) designata da Andronico Cireste, reportata nell' Architettura di Vitruvio.

Il Tempio di Teseo.

I Fondamenti dell' Areopago.

Prima di cadere in mano de' Veneti era popolata da otto a nove mila abitanti, di questi tre parti erano Greci, gli altri Turchi che aveano quattro moschee nella Città, e una nel Castello. Quivi non erano tolerati gli Ebrei, non essendo gli Ateniesi meno di loro accorti et astuti; onde correa Proverbio: "Dio ci guardi dagl' Ebrei di Salonichio, dalli Greci d' Atene, e dai Turchi di Negroponte." Vestivano questi Greci differentemente dai Turchi, portando vesti nere alquanto strette. Conservavano un non so che di civile e politico con qualche retaggio dell' antichità. Inclinati alle lettere più che all' armi deliciavano tra le libere conversazioni, procurando di mantenersi co' Turchi al più possibile. Questa città è antichissma e fu madre del sapere, scuola di Marte, ed Accademia universale delle virtù. Tale fiorì avanti la nascità di Cristo, e si conservò nel suo decoro lungo tempo. Passò con gli anni al comando di varij Principi perchè i moltiplici accidenti così la constrinsero. Silla doppo d' averla con lungo assedio tentata si fece padrone, allor che retrovavasi all' ubbidienza d' Aristonico, Epicureo filosofo, tiranno. Fu trionfo di Baiazette Secondo, indi ottenutola Renier Acciaioli la diede alla Republica Veneta. Ritornò ciò non ostante in poter degli Acciaioli medesimi, che signoreggiavano l' Attica e la Beotia. Nell' anno 1455 assediata da Maometto Secondo fu dal detto presa per mancanza de' soccorsi, e durò sotto la tirannide Ottomana sino quest' anno, che tornò al dominio de' Veneti in meno di giorni otto senza pure costasse a medesimi nè sangue nè fattica,[20] ancorchè non mancasse il Seraschiero di tentare la diversione con grossa partita di cavalli, che alla semplice vista delle Venete schiere fu obligata da queste a vergognosa fuga.[21]

Correa si formidabile il nome del Capitan Generale Morosini che per timore s' abbandonavano i Turchi ad ogni partito per isfuggire i cimenti, parendo loro acquistar gloria dall' esser vinti da lui.[22] Ebbe il Morosini la gloria di soggettar nello stesso tempo, alla fama del suo temuto nome, e Misitrà, che fu l' antica Sparta, e Atene la Famosa; a distruggione delle quali guidò Serse un milion de' guerrieri; ma trovò che se li oppose Leonida a Termopile, e Temistocle in quei mari, costretto alla fine tornar in Persia senza essercito e senz' onore.

[Doppo l' acquisto d'Atene però scuopertasi in Misitrà la peste, furono d' ordine di Sua Eccellenza sequestrati i Turchi, levando loro il commercio sino alla nuova stagione per non ischerzare coi pericoli di questo epidemico male.] [23]

I Turchi di Megara, documentati dall' esempio degli altri, per non soccombere al destino d' una resa a discrezione abbandonarono il luogo, e perchè non tornasse a riabitarsi da quei Barbari, ordinò Sua Eccellenza fosse incendiato, restando anco questa terza reliquia d' antichità sepolta nelle sue ruine.[24] Acciochè sopraviva al loro nome anco la memoria, in questo istorico registro non s' ommette qualche notizia loro, giachè le ricerca il fatto.

Misitrà fu prima detta Sparta, poi Lacedemone, città famossissima della Grecia.[25] Fu si vasta ne' proprij recinti che a' tempi di Polibio girava 48 stadij in figura quasi rotonda, sopra sito parte erto e parte giacente. Passata con l' antichità dall' ampiezza all' angustie, si conserva in questo secolo ristretta in picciola terra. Vive solo insepolto il fasto delle memorabili sue glorie dalle vestigia che apariscono. Per ottocento anni sprovista di mura si mantenne che poi più volte le furono aggiunte, come si vede che la stessa terra ed il Castello si trova delle stesse munito, ma debolamente. Ha due gran' Porte, quella da settentrione conduce a Napoli di Romania e l' altra da levante al Borgo di fuori. Quattro sono le parti che la dividono, formando però tutte assiemme un corpo senza gionture. Il Castello una, la Terra l' altra, e due Borghi, l' uno chiamato Mesokorion, cioè Borgo di mezzo; Exokorion è l' altro, cioè Borgo di fuori. Questo Exokorion è separato dalle tre altre parti per il fiume Vasolipotamos; quindi a quelle s' unisce per un sol ponte di pietra.

È nel sito si vantaggioso questo propugnacolo che, per quale si ricava dalle storie, non è stato mai sorpreso a forza d' armi benchè tentato da Meemet Secondo e da' Veneti. Fu fabricato nella declinazione dell' Imperio Greco per opera di despoti; perchè un altro eretto sopra la collina opposta, del quale appariscono tutta via le rovine, non dominava sufficientemente la città. Passò questo luogo al dominio di varij despoti sinchè per fatalità fu rapito da Maometto Secondo negli anni in circa 1465, facendo segar a mezzo il Governatore del Castello.[26] Poi Benedetto Colleone, pugnando per la Republica, 1473 la vinse, et averebbe espugnato anco il Castello, se nel mentre cercava il trionfo non fosse rimasto ucciso.[27] Questo anno 1687 scosse il giogo de' Barbari e respirò all' aura della libertà Veneta.

Megara poi egualmente distante 26 miglia da Corinto e da Atene, vanta nell' Accaia sopra l' eminenza d' un colle il suo antico sito. Il suo Borgo si compone d' un numero mediocre di case, fabricate per lo più di pietra cotta, coperte di bachette assodate coll' impasto di certa terra a tal effetto usuale. I nazionali sono Greci, ma era abitata anco da Turchi.[28] Ebbe anticamente titolo di città capitale del territorio Megarese; confinante con Eleusine era degli Ateniesi doviziosa porzione. Vi è un porto picciolo lungi due miglia dal Borgo, posto nell' ultimo recesso del Golfo d' Engia, qual servì di stazione alle navi Megaresi. A settentrione di questo luogo sono nella pianura varie chiese de' Greci,[29] d' intorno alle quale v' era in altri tempi una villa detta Paleocoria, oggidì desolata e distrutta. Se l' antichità non portasse seco le ruine, si vederebbero anco al giorno d' oggi quelle fabriche, che furono pompa onorata a città cotanto illustre, quali con tutte che siano dannate dal tempo a morder l' erbe innocenti, fanno nulla di meno a passaggieri a quest' ora inchiodar su quelle scheggie fatali instupidito il guardo.

Eravi aggiunto alla singolarità delle sue magnificenze l'edificio d' una fonte in cui accoppiati si vedeano gli ultimi sforzi dell' arte. Da questa non molto lungi campeggiò un tempio nel quale scolpite l' imagini delli dodici dei di mano di Prassitele coll' effigie degli Imperatori formavano maravigliosa galeria del mondo. Quivi pure si conservava la statua di bronzo, che rappresentava Diana inalzata da' Megaresi, e intitolata Salvatrice loro; avendosi preservati, comme follemente credeano, dall' essercito di Mardonio, che smarrita la via di notte tempo, supponendo campo nemico una montagna, e scarricando sopra la medesima quanti stromenti militari avea, rimasto senz' armi, fu combattuto dagli armati Megaresi e vinto. Seguiva indi il tempio consegrato a Giove Olympico con la statua d' oro e d' avorio che non restò perficionata a causa delle guerre che ebbero con i

Peloponnesi, nello stesso modo ritrovandosi imperfette alcune altre opere di gran spesa che servir doveano d' ornamento all' accennata statua; in quella parte appunto ove stava appalo in trofeo lo sprone di rame d' una galea tolta agli Ateniesi, allora che i nazionali di Megara tentarono ricuperare, come fecero, l' isola di Salamine, che se gli era ribellata. Doppo d' essere passata dal falso culto dell' idolatria a quello empio di Maometto venne coll' incendio comandato dal Morosini il mese d' Ottobre purificato quel terreno degli impuri sacrificij per rinascere alla Fede Cattolica col respiro della fortunata pace.

Di tutti questi felicissimi successi seguiti in corso di due mesi poco più raguagliò il Generalissimo intieramente il Senato, e spedì sopra una tartana Capitano Fabbio Zonca, [chi] era suo Capitano di Guardia,[30] a finchè la Republica comprendesse il fervore del di lui zelo verso l' ingrandimento della Patria, e s' appagasse dell' instancabile attenzione sua ai progressi maggiori dell' armi ben impiegate, e accogliesse col gradimento i frutti d' una generosa e prudente condotta, con intenzione principale di promovere nell' animo di ciascheduno, che insisteva al governo risoluzioni generose di rinforzare con la nuova spedizione di milizie l' essercito diminuito dalle infermità, fattiche, e patimenti si lunghi; e particolarmente dalla necessità di presidiare le piazze ed i luoghi acquistati; onde alla nuova stagione si potesse intraprender qualche impresa considerabile, e prosseguir la guerra col vantaggio, e con l' aura di tante gloriose vittorie donate da Dio a consolazione del Cristianesimo.

[The narrative now turns to the movements of the Imperial armies in southeastern Hungary.]

CHAPTER III

The Abandonment of Athens

[This extract [1] is preceded by an account of the determination of the Venetians to prosecute the war during 1688 in both Greece and Dalmatia, while maintaining peace and prosperity at home.]

Il Capitan Generale Morosini doppo l'acquisto d' Atene si fermò con una parte dell' armata maritima in Porto Lion e con la terestre in Atene allogiata in quel Borgo.[2] Durò per molto tempo a quella parte placida la stagione con gran solievo delle milizie, così per l' esenzione che godeano dai patimenti come per la comodità che s' avea di dar la concia con minor spesa e più prestezza all' armata.[3] Finalmente con la nuova luna al fin di Genaro cadendo d'improviso gran quantità di neve fece tali freddi che travagliarono molto i corpi con varie infermità. Causò questo sconcerto de' tempi una borasca pericolosa che l' agitò l' armata nel Porto; ma nel Golfo di Corinto fattasi sentire più furiosa fece naufragare infelicemente gli vascelli Imperator Leopoldo e Tre Re, quello Raguseo e questo dalla decima di Cefalonia, ambidue noleggiati, e durò molto a salvarsi da questo disastro la nave Apparizione, sopra la quale era l'Almirante Zaguri, col tagliare gli alberi, e la perdita suddetta non seguì senza qualche perdita di persone. In aggiunta di questo infortunio seguì anco nel porto di Cerigo il naufragio della nave Quattro Fratelli, molto poderosa e bella, senza essersi trovato altro segno di essa che una gomena col danno della gente e delle publiche provisioni.[4] Inoltratosi in tanto fuori d' Atene sotto la direzione del Sargente Maggiore di Battaglia, Lauro Darduino, che commandava la nazione oltramarina, con 300 soldati di questa in partita per due giornate nel paese nemico sortì a lui l' incontro d' alcuni

Turchi, e parte truccidati, parte fatti schiavi, fecero preda considerabile d' animali che servirono a reparo del bissogno in cui si trovava l'armata.[5]

Considerando l' Eccellenza del Capitan Generale quanto inutile sarebbe stato il mantenere in Atene qualche presidio col pericolo che questa fortezza potesse essere travagliata dal Seraschiero della Morea in occasione che l' armi publiche fossero impegnate in qualche assedio importante, oltre il beneficio che averebbe riportato il riguardo publico di rendere con quei abitanti abitate le città della Morea et accresciuto il numero di milizie con quei si disponessero d' arrolarsi, venne in deliberazione di portar al Senato le sue riflessioni in tempo che in Venezia v' era chi essibiva a nome d' Atheniesi qualche somma di denaro per redur quella piazza in istato di difesa. Riportò nulla di meno tutta l' autorità per far ciò che avesse stimato più conferente al ben publico. In ordine a che fu abbandonata essa piazza nel suo essere, con lo trasporto del cannone e munizioni. Furono levati gli abitanti, e fatti trasportare, parte nelle città della Morea, particolarmente in Napoli Romania, e parte al Zante; fermandosi le gente ordinarie con l'armi a Corinto dove, allogiate le loro famiglie, dissegnavano di voler accumunarsi con quei di quel regno per condursi a danneggiare il comun nemico.[6] In questo modo restò disertata[7] l' antica Atene, che sino all' ora s' avea continuata con qualche decoro e fortuna migliore tra tutte le città della Grecia per quello le permetteva il barbaro dominio de' Turchi. [Poco fortunato acquisto riuscì questo alle vittorie del Morosini, mentre in avvenire parve che il Genio tutelare di questa città quasi distrutta, conspirante con una fatalità aperta in vendetta, cercasse d' opponersi nemico alle di lui generose risoluzioni.][8]

Nello stesso tempo corse la medesima sorte Misitrà, l' antica Sparta; mentre i Turchi, già resi l' autunno decorso a discrezione et ivi trattenuti l' inverno a causa di qualche sospetto che correa di mal contaggioso, s' intendevano con la piazza di Napoli di Malvasia, e fecero rissolvere il Capitan Generale di farli marchiare con le necessarie custodie tutti con le loro famiglie in Argo per togliere loro questa occasione, lasciando ai Mainotti il luogo suddetto da essi bramato per il passo libero di loro maggiore sicurezza e comodo.

Si restituirono in questo mentre al Porto Lion verso i primi Febraio il Governatore de' Navi, Imperial Contarini, e le sue conserve doppo d' aversi trattenute alle crociere del Canal di Negroponte sino verso qui sbandate dal tempo, e a mezzo il mese la squadra del Capitan Straordinario, Lorenzo Veniero.[9] All' arrivo di lui volendosi in atto di complimentare portarsi i capi da mar, Proveditor d' Armata Garzoni, Capitan Straordinario delle Galeazze Querini, e Governatore de' Condennati Pisani, in una felucca, loro successe nel calar la vela di ribaltarsi, e non fu poco, che li marinari esistessero in loro ayiuto, essendo lontani da terra un miglio in più, e che si salvassero, mentre nè il Querini nè il Pisani sapevano nuotare. Sortì loro di ridursi tutti sopra il fondo della felucca, stando in gran pericolo, se non venivano presto soccorsi da una delle felucche Napolitane, che aversa colà gli salvò la vita. Anco il nipote dell' Eccellenza del Capitan Generale qualche giorno prima, stando in una delle felucche medesime e per la violenza della voga mancatole il piede, andò in acqua e a fondo, e tornato miracolosamente sopra fu ricuperato. A che passo riducono le inconsiderazioni! Fu ottimo instituto degli antichi Romani che la loro gioventù apprendesse a nuotar prima d' intraprender governi maritimi in servizio della Patria.

Spedite a Napoli Romania undici galere trovarono quella e l' altre piazze del Regno libere d' ogni sospetto e i lavori ben avanzati, particolarmente quello della gran scala che dalla sommità della Fortezza calava verso il mare e serviva per gli soccorsi in caso di qualche attacco.[10] Prima di portarsi il Capitan Generale al Porto Poro come più comodo di far l' imbarco delle milizie e d' allestirsi alla mossa dell' iminente campeggiamento, ordinò che si terminasse la miserabile tragedia di quei di Misitrà, provedamente di già trasportati in Argos.[11] Ivi ricevuti sotto la custodia del Proveditor in Regno Benzon sopra quattro marciliane a questo effetto mandate in quel porto, fu cosa curiosa a vederli in numero di due mila marchiare con loro drappi da uso, seguiti da un gran numero d' animali da somma con bagaglio di qualche valore. Persone anco molto civili, donne, ragazzi s' udivano a lamentarsi col destino di così dolorosa necessità di mutar luogo e condizione. Al numero di 280 in circa successe il bene di farsi Cristiani, gli altri però furono condotti al grande scoglio di Tolone, lontano da Napoli di Romania sei miglia; ove fatti sbarcare con le loro robbe, furono scelti 770 buoni da remo e destinati al servizio delle galere, eccettuato il Bassa, che restò come schiavo in deposito. Li putti e le putte furono compartite per i capi dell' armata, e le donne e i vecchi lasciati in libertà. Questi miserabili vedendo attaccarsi da loro li detti destinati per le galere diedero in pianti e gemiti, nè vi mancò chi per soverchia passione si getasse disperatamente in mare. Assistevano i capi da mar alla raccolta delle robbe e alla cerca di ciò che altro potea trovarsi. Il tutto fu riposto ne' sacchi e sigillato per essere diviso per tutta l' armata. Le notte dei 5 Marzo furono fatte rimurchiar le marciliane inviando le donne e i vecchi in paese de' Turchi, alcuni restando trattenuti per far cambio, se occorresse, coi schiavi Christiani. Quanto diverso destino vidde questo secolo di questi due miserabili avanzi dell' antichità, di quello aveano veduti gli Ateniesi e gli Spartani in tempo che fiorirono queste loro famose patrie. Anco le città e i regni sono destinati a morire, e tutto quello ha principio quaggiù, ha parimente il suo fine.

Le cose de' Turchi in quella parte caminavano pure assai confuse e senz' alcun ordine di poter comparire in qualche positura per l' entrante campagna. Per le notizie che teneva il Capitan Generale il Seraschiero si trovava a Cariso ai confini dell' Arta [12] con pochissima gente col dubbio d' essere rimosso dalla carica, vociferandosi che li potesse essere sostituito Say Bassa [13] che teneva qualche seguito de' suoi, dichiarato Visir della Morea, quello che con li soldati andò a Costantinopoli per la riforma del Governo; ma continuavano in quella reggia più che mai le turbolenze, e s' andava sbandando di giorno in giorno l' esercito colà comparso per andar in Ungheria. Da che appariva chiaramente che non erano in istato i Turchi di radunare alcuno corpo valido di gente che potesse resistere all' armi Venete in caso intraprendessero qualche attacco.[14] Aveano in quell' arsenale dato mano a fabricare 40 galeotte di 80 leventi [15] per cadauna per valersi a far diversione ai Veneti in Levante, apprestando a furia legni per detto effetto; ma si stimò impossibile che per quella campagna potessero trovare gente pratica per condurle et assuefatta al mare; onde si sperava che sarebbe stato inutile questo loro solecito travaglio. V' erano pure seguito alcune solevazioni tra' Bulgari [16] nelle attenenze di Salonicchio, alle quali s' ingegnava la Porta Ottomana di provedere, avendo mandato un Bassa con seguito per rimettere, se poteano, al servizio quei 500 soldati che destinati per guarniggione in Negroponte aveano il passato inverno con violenze voluto tornare alle loro case, ricusando di star chiusi con tanto incomodo loro e patimento in quella piazza, che più d' ogni altra temeva il vicino assedio.[17] Dissegnavano pure di spinger qualche numero di londre con le necessarie provisioni a Napoli di Malvasia, esposta già ai travagli e pericoli, venendole vietata al possibile ogni entrata di soccorsi.

Al Porto Porro [18] era destinata la raccolta dell' armi, e

ivi erano dirizzate tutte le spedizioni delle truppe e navigli, come più comodo alle mosse che di già andava concependo la mente instancabile del Capitan Generale, incaricato dal Governo d' impiegarsi con tutte le forze ove averebbe stimato più proffittevole l' azzardo; mentre non si mancava di solecitare a tutto potere l' arrivo delle milizie Alemanne, Svizzere, ed Italiane al Lido per darle opportuno imbarco.

[La sapienza publica applicò i riflessi non meno agli affari di guerra che a quelli di Stato per ricavare con le notizie di questi i vantaggi e frutti di quelli. Destinò dunque a questa causa tre Sindici Catasticatori nel Regno della Morea per dar principio all' osservazione degli acquisti per ridurli alle debite contribuzioni, e furono tre gravissimi Senatori, Domenico Gritti, Girolimo Renier e Marino Michiel.] [19]

Ranuccio 2, Duca di Parma, concorse a dar al soldo della Republica fanti 450, fatti condurre per il Po con i loro ufficiali, in testimonio di amore e stima già professata ereditaria a quel publico.[20] Passò nell' armata Nobile Huomo Polo Nani per Commissario a dar cambio all' Emo, eletto dal Pontefice in Arcivescovo di Corfù in luogo del Cardinale Barbarigo, proveduto del Vescovato di Monte Fiascon.[21] La necessità, che tolse a sì importante carica soggetto di tanta integrità e zelo verso il publico servizio, rese molto sconsolata la Republica in quel urgentissimo bissogno, che ricercava la continuazione di lui per la prattica desterità e maniere caritatevoli che valsero renderlo applausibile in quell' impiego per altro di tutta gelosia e circonspirizione.

In questo tempo che la stessa Republica era solecita nelle spedizioni opportune e nelle risoluzioni necessarie per la nuova campagna, si infermò il Serenissimo Marc Antonio Giustiniano al principio della stagione, e in poco più di giorni quindici di infermità, non capita da' medici, terminò il corso della sua vita la vigilia dell' Annonciazione della Beata Vergine con universal condoglio.[22] Morì in età di 69 anni doppo d' esser stato nel Principato anni quattro e mesi due, glorioso per tante vittorie ottenute dall' armi publiche nella Morea e nella Dalmazia, molto contento dell' imprese segnalate concesse da Dio a Leopoldo Cesare collegato con la Republica. Il di lui principato fu solennissimo per le successive feste seguite a causa dei felici progressi della Lega ad oppressione de' Barberi, e passò dalle allegrezze del mondo Cattolico all' immarcessibili glorie e godimenti eterni di Paradiso, mercè alla rettitudine delle sue intenzionali verso il ben della Patria e della Cristianità, alla compostezza d' un animo religiosissimo con cui s' è mostrato sempre da privato e da prencipe, alla saviezza con cui s' è diportato nelle cariche publiche con molto decoro e con gran genio benefico verso i sudditi. Fu al vivo compianta la di lui morte da tutti con sospiri di devozione e tenerezza verso quella grand' anima, nè si puòle lasciar partir da questa alla miglior vita senza opinione di santità, avendolo Dio in questo mondo distinto da tutti i Prencipi precessori con tante felicità de' successi da lui incontrate sempre con umiltà di ringraziamenti a Dio in publico et in privato esemplarij e meritorij, et era chiamato per antonomasia il Doge delle Vittorie, e dei *Te Deum*.

Terminate le di lui pompe funerali con le formalità praticate, si devenne con gli ordini prescritti all' elezione del di lui successore.[23] Passò per tutti gli scrutinij a stabilirsi nel quaranta uno numero eletticco del Principato il nome maestoso del Generalissimo Francesco Morosini senza concorenza, e ne rimase a tutti i voti, persuaso tutto il corpo patricio ad esaltarlo a dignità così sublime per le sue insigni benemerenze formate in lui da una instancabile applicazione agli acquisti in quatro successive campagne con tanto publico beneficio e decoro. Si publicò la di lui dignissima elezione li tre Aprile, solemnizata per tre sere con gran fuochi, machine, et apparati di varia invenzione, di molta spesa, lode, e sodisfazione d' un infinito concorso.[24] Varij concetti corsero intorno questo ellettivo successo in cui non si pratticarono le solite concorrenze, ma si videro concordati tutti i voleri in un solo. Ebbe a dir un Ministro di gran Principe in un luogo cospicuo prima che venisse praticata la sudetta elezione nella persona del Generalissimo sudetto, " Molti dicono che è ben a farlo, e molti che non è bene; ma tutti concludono che è necessità di farlo." [25]

[There follows a brief mention of the dispatch of Zuccati, a secretary of the Pregadi, to Morosini with the letter of the Senate announcing his election, the Beretta Ducale, and the Formulario. After an account of Cornaro's preparations in Dalmatia for an attack on Knin, the volume ends abruptly with a few pages on the movements of the Imperial army, and the plans of the Turks for the defence of Belgrade.]

APPENDICES

APPENDIX I

Turenne

Louis de La Tour d'Auvergne, Prince de Turenne, son of Godefroy-Maurice, Duc de Bouillon, and great-nephew of Marshal Turenne, had obtained in 1685 the permission of Louis XIV to join the Polish army with his two cousins, the young princes of Conti, in the war against the Turks. On their arrival in Germany, however, they were persuaded to make the campaign with the imperial forces in Hungary under the command of Charles of Lorraine, and distinguished themselves at the battle of Grau and the siege of Neuhausel. By this readiness to serve under a general who was the King's sworn enemy, they inevitably incurred the royal displeasure, and Turenne soon after fell into complete disgrace when, with other members of his family, he became gravely involved in the scandal of the Conti letters.[1] Forbidden to enter France without permission and rightly believing that further service with the Emperor would only add to his offense, Turenne now turned toward Venice, for as Zipoli, the Florentine agent in Paris, wrote to Secretary Gondi, " non nascondono qui il piacere che hanno de' progressi de' Venetiani et parimente il disgusto delli avantaggi dell' Imperatore." [2]

On his arrival in April, 1686, accompanied by a numerous train of gentlemen, he was received with great distinction by the Republic, which granted him, according to Teglia, " un legno espresso a sua disposizione per l' imbarco di sè stesso, e sue camerate al numero di 20, ciascuna con un servitore." [3] He responded to this honor by drawing from Paris 100,000 scudi for his expenses,[4]—a clear indication that he proposed, although only a " Venturiere " without official rank, to maintain a state in accordance with the wealth and position of his family. That he was also determined to maintain fully its military reputation was proved at the opening of the campaign by his conduct at the battle before Navarino Nuovo,[5] while his further services during the course of the summer led to a public demonstration of approval on his return to Venice after the surrender of Nauplia, "con nobile rinfresco mandatogli all' abitazione numeroso di molti bacili pieni di varij comestibili."[6] In the following year he played such a prominent part in the victory at Patras that the Senate voted him a jewelled sword worth 2400 ducats.[7] The siege of the Acropolis naturally afforded him little opportunity for distinction, but we are told that during the first night in the olive grove, "il Generale (*i. e.* Königsmark) con li Principi di Bransvich e Turena sino al spuntar dell' aurora girarono il campo per osservare se si vegliava opportunamente."[8]

It would seem that during these two years in the field he had shown qualities which led his friends to believe that in spite of his youth—he was only twenty-three—he was fitted to hold an important command, since on his return to Venice for the winter the Senate decided to offer commissions as "Tenente-Generale di Fanteria in Levante" to Turenne and Prince Maximilian of Brunswick-Lüneburg,[9] and a month later Guasconi wrote to Florence: "Sabato sera in Senato fu condotto il Signor Principe di Turena con titolo di Generale come il Signor Principe Massimiliano di Bransvich, ma con 5000 ducati solamente di stipendio dove l' altro ne ha 6000, e con condizione trovandosi insieme di ricevere gl' ordini da Bransvich, e ne ha spedito corriere a Parigi per ricavarne l' assenso da Sua Maestà."[10] The offer was a tempting one, for the Senate was at this time looking for "un Generale subalterno che possa supplire in difetto di Kinismarch,"[11] and it seems likely that the two young princes would have ranked as second in command. To the Venetian request, duly transmitted by the French ambassador, as also to Turenne's petition, Louis made no reply; and Turenne's family, who were still excluded from the Court, considering that in this case silence certainly did *not* give consent, advised him to refuse the offer.[12] He therefore decided to continue his service as "Venturiere," and on June 23, 1688, arrived at Poros with forty gentlemen, double the number which had accompanied him two years before.[13]

Although wounded in the arm during an attack on the Turkish outworks at Negroponte,[14] he remained with the army until the abandonment of the siege, when he returned to Italy.[15] The next year furnished no opportunity for active service, and in the autumn he joined his uncle, the Cardinal de Bouillon, at Rome. In 1690 Louis at last relented, the Duke and Duchess of Bouillon were permitted to return to the Court, and on November 23 Turenne was received by the king and speedily restored to favor, for in 1691 we find him, as "aide-de-camp du Roi" winning special praise for his excellent reports on the operations before Mons and Namur. His brilliant and promising career was cut short by his death on August 4, 1692, from wounds received at the battle of Steenkirk.[16]

APPENDIX II

Mistra

What Ivanovich well calls "la miserabile tragedia di quei di Misitrà" proved throughout the autumn and winter for Morosini, in his own words, a "molestissimo imbarazzo," from which he finally freed himself, at no small cost to his reputation, by a cold-blooded severity, which was very close to a breach of faith and was condemned even by contemporaries accustomed to the cruelties of the Turkish wars.

After the battle of Patras and the flight of the Turkish army from the Morea, the garrison of Mistra, which had hitherto refused to submit even though the Venetians were masters of all the southern Peloponnesus except Monemvasia, finding themselves attacked by Nicolò Polani, Proveditor of Zarnata, at the head of a band of Mainiotes and cut off from all hope of relief, sent envoys to Morosini at Corinth offering to surrender, if they were granted favorable terms. On August eighteenth, however, the Council of War decided that after so prolonged a resistance their repentance came too late to entitle them to any consideration, and " si dovesse perciò convenire, che rimanendo in schiavitù gl' habili tutti al servizio del remo, si lasciassero partir poi le donne, putti, e vecchi, che surpassero li 50 anni, coll' altre accessorie circonstanze in essa Consulta dichiarite." Accordingly the envoys were sent back with a letter setting forth these severe terms, but adding that they could purchase their complete liberty by paying to the public treasury a ransom of two hundred thousand reali in coin, gold, jewels, and silver.[1] On his voyage around the Peloponnesus Morosini stopped at Porto Vathi to receive a large delegation bringing the reply from Mistra. The Turks declared that they could not pay any such ransom, although Muazzo, a very bitter critic of Morosini's treatment of Mistra, believed that while the amount was certainly large, it was not beyond their resources.[2] Garzoni says that they offered instead to leave all their belongings behind and depart " coperti solamente con povero grigio," and that this offer would have been accepted, but for a report that the plague had appeared in Mistra.[3] The Council of War, thereupon, ordered that they should surrender their arms and horses to Polani and remain in strict quarantine until free from all suspicion of contagion, " per dover all' hora poi dispender la sorte loro, salve le sole vite, dalle prescrittioni di questa carica e da quegl' atti gratiosi, che sono indivisibili dalla generosa clemenza della Serenità Vostra."[4] An agreement on these terms was signed and sealed, and Morosini sent back four of the envoys to see that the conditions were fulfilled, while thirty-two others were placed, as hostages, in quarantine on a " marciliana."[5]

The presence of plague in Mistra was confirmed soon after Morosini's arrival at Athens, and he promptly regulated the distribution of millet to the quarantined inhabitants, " con ordine che sia in effettivo contante pagato in cassa pubblica il valor della predetta dispensa, e che dalla gente comoda sia la miserabile soccorsa e proveduta."[6] Since, because of the strict quarantine, food could only be obtained from the Venetians, this order naturally produced great discontent, not a little suffering, and various attempts to evade its restrictions. Even before serious trouble arose Morosini felt the need of a speedy settlement, for on December seventeenth he wrote to the Senate: " Mentre poi mi sta troppo a cuore, che si dia compimento all' imbrogliata e lunga facenda di Mistrà, credo pensando levar di là quella gente, e col trattener sopra vascelli in contumacia gl' habili al remo, far traghettare in alcun luogho della terra ferma le donne coi figli, perchè in altra maniera mai si potrà sviluppare si fastidioso imbarazzo, apparendo ancora segni contaggiosi per le inquisitioni dall' Illustrissimo Signor Proveditor Benzon rilevati."

At this time, however, the future of Athens called for immediate discussion, and apparently it was not until January twenty-second that the Council of War, aroused by a report from Benzon on the grave disorders which had recently developed, ordered him to move at once all the Turks to Argos and thence transport them by sea to the rocky promontory of Tolon, where they were to be kept in strict quarantine until Morosini's plan for their disposal could safely be carried out. To this command the Turks of the lower town promptly submitted. Those of the castle at first refused, but after a brief resistance were easily forced by Benzon to yield. They now begged for pardon, but unfortunately for them it was found that they had not surrendered all their arms as required by the terms granted at Porto Vathi.[7] Accordingly the Council of War, held on March second after Morosini's arrival at Nauplia, decided that their crimes were so great that they had forfeited all claim to consideration and must be punished by much harsher treatment than had been originally promised. The minutes of the Council of War and Morosini's letter from Athens on March nineteenth set forth the Venetian case in great detail. It appears that the " enorme deliquenze," which warranted disregard of the earlier agreement, consisted in the concealment of arms, stealing millet from the public stores, burning houses in the city, leaving the town for Monemvasia in breach of quarantine, and especially in refusing to surrender the castle " con turpe mancamento di fede "; for all which offenses they were certainly guilty of " Lesa Maestà," and justly deserved the terrible sentence reported by Ivanovich and more briefly by the *Avvisi*.

On one point, however, there was an important difference between the decision of the Council as announced in Venice, and as actually voted and executed. According to Ivanovich the women and old men were to be " lasciati in libertà " and were with few exceptions actually taken by the ships " in paese de' Turchi." The *Avvisi* say that they were to be sent from Tolon to Monemvasia " per maggiormente indurre quella piazza in carestia de' viveri." [8] In reality the Council decided that they should be taken to Athens to be exchanged for Christian soldiers enslaved at Negroponte and elsewhere at the rate of two or more Turkish women for one Christian. Morosini gives the total number of prisoners as 2420,[9] from whom 778 men between 16 and 50 years of age were at once sent to the galleys, while 312 boys and girls, after having been baptized in accordance with the orders of the Council, were distributed as slaves among the officers of the fleet and army. The rest, after having been thoroughly searched for anything of value, were embarked for Athens on five ships, which were at first towed by the galleys. A violent tramontana, however, made it impossible for the fleet to advance beyond Poros; indeed it became necessary to return to Castri under the shelter of Cape Thermia, where Morosini left the five " marciliane " with orders to await better weather, while he himself continued the voyage with the galleys, which reinforced by the new slaves from Mistra were able to disregard the gale.[10]

He reached Athens by March thirteenth, but as late as March twenty-eighth the Council of War was anxiously awaiting the arrival of the ships, which were needed to transport the army to Poros. They must have arrived soon after, since the army left on April eighth, but there had certainly been no time, and apparently no attempt, to arrange any exchange of prisoners. None the less in his long letter of April fifteenth from Porto Poro Morosini, in the midst of his anxieties about the health of the army, consoled himself, " d' esser felicemente uscito doppo gagliardi e lunghi contrasti dall' imbarazzo stesso coll' haver pure com-partito all' armata di mar e di terra li 312 putti di minor età, previa l' estrattione spettante alla decima di Vostri Signori, et al sesso femminile poi d' ogni età, che sarebbe stato di perniciosissimo inutile ingombro, e che partorir solo poteva pessimi effetti in ogn' ordine di questi militanti, fatto sù le rive di Porto Lion sbarcare nel procinto, che di là si staccava l' armata, le rilasciai a maggior confusione de' nemici, et a cospicuo lustro dell' invitta gloriosa grandezza della Serenità Vostra il passoporto, che in copia inserisco, dandomi pur a credere, che di crucioso peso riuscirà certo a' Turchi l' obbligo di non abbandonare sì miserabile gente, da cui finalmente non le può che un molestissimo disturbo derivare." Comment on such an attitude is surely needless.

This final act of the tragedy does not seem to have been generally known at Venice. We have seen that both Ivanovich and the *Avvisi* assume that the women and old men had been set at liberty in Turkish territory, and this was also the belief of Garzoni, whose history was licensed as late as 1705. Even Matteo del Teglia, no friend to Morosini and after the disaster at Negroponte more than ready to enlarge on all his faults, has no hint of blame for his treatment of Mistra. Yet this feeling was not universal in Venice, for Garzoni thus concludes his account of this episode: " Della descritta sentenza speculazioni sinistre ne formò il Mondo, ò ignaro del fatto, ò con la regola fallacissima de gli accidenti posteriormente veduti. Siccome è riserbata al Cielo l' approvazione delle imprese, così de gli eventi impenetrabile à gl' occhi nostri la vera cagione e il metodo de gli abissi. Molti imputarono al cambiamento de' patti con Mistrà quello della fortuna; altri alla morte del Doge Giustiniani, Principe di rare parti." [11] Even here, however, it is the breach of the original terms of surrender rather than the treatment of the prisoners that has called for Divine chastisement.[12]

APPENDIX III

The Withdrawal of the Army from Athens

We have seen that just before leaving Corinth Morosini had somewhat suddenly concluded that Athens could not be held without a much stronger force than would be available when active operations were resumed. The outbreak of plague in the Morea, which led to the decision on October second to keep the army in Athens for the winter,[1] made it possible to defer immediate consideration of the fate of the city, but on December thirty-first Morosini, after consulting Königsmark, brought the question in all its aspects before the Council of War.[2] It was the unanimous opinion that there was neither time nor money to construct permanent fortifications around the lower town, and that the inhabitants must be deported to save them from the Turks, but that the houses should be left standing, so that the Greeks might not feel that they were cut off from all hope of return. Two days later, on January second,[3] the Council was told that the plague was rife in the Morea and that there were suspicions of its presence in Athens, and it was at once decided to beg the Greeks to leave, so that the army might also be withdrawn from danger of infection.

These decisions were submitted to the Senate by Morosini in his letter of January sixth.[4] After the passage quoted by Laborde, ending with the words " barbarie de' nemici," the letter continues: " Firmata la deliberatione predeta col più vivo compatimento verso la costitutione di queste benemerite genti s' hebbe anco pietoso riguardo al possibil loro sollievo, onde fu inoltre dichiarito farli trasportare in alcuna parte della Morea, et assegnarle modo sufficiente al vivere de' più bisognosi, così che riconoscano la paterna predilettione della Serenità Vostra nel sovvenire alle loro indigenze, come dalla copia della Consulta distintamente apparisce. Fatti chiamare perciò alla mia presenza i Primati, e partecipatogli quanto s' era divisato di praticare per consolatione e servitio loro commune, li vado tutta via istillando con dolcezza l' accomodarsi alla necessità, che così vuole, et a ricevere con buona sofferenza il cambiamento della sorte, a che Dio Signore li destina, mentre della Santa Sua Providenza e delle assistenze caritatevoli del più religioso Principe del Mondo non puon' mai diffidare. Mentre però sono ancora perplessi e confusi nel prescieglier il luogo da ricovrarsi in Morea, succede, che a maggiore stordimento loro e mio più fastidioso imbarazzo si intenda, sparsa in varie parti d' esso Regno l' apparenza del morbo infesto."

The contents of this letter caused the Venetian government much anxiety, not only on account of the reappearance of the plague in the Morea, but as Teglia said, " più di tutto il tenore delle ultime del Signor Capitano Generale che rappresenta la resolutione di demolire Atene."[5] Guasconi, who had reported on February fourth the receipt of the letter of January sixth and the plan to remove the Athenians,[6] wrote on the seventh that the Senate had determined to reply to Morosini that they would regret the destruction of Athens and the abandonment of such a pleasant country, but that they would leave the decision in his hands, only " raccomandoli in tal caso di assistere e ben trattare quei benemerenti popoli, e dargli larga ricompensa di terreni e abitationi in Morea."[7] This recommendation was in accord with the feelings of Morosini, who seems to have regretted sincerely the measures which he felt compelled to take, and on March eighteenth wrote to the Senate, " conturbate però tutte queste genti dal fatal destino, che con misera condittione le forza per hora snidarsi dalla patria, cade necessariamente anco la raggione d'astringerle a rilasciar il già patuito tributo, se anzi non posso che al vivo compatirle, et assister caritatevolmente all' infelicità dell' attual suo stato."[8]

The Inquisitori di Stato were silent on this topic until the *Avviso* of March thirteenth, which reported that letters of February second from Athens, after describing the construction of a wall and trench across the peninsula of the Piraeus,[9] continued: " Si erano fatti varii progetti per il quid inde d'Atene vastissima di case; e come il fortificarne qualche portione niente vale, e così non potendosi fare il molto, restavano persuasi quei habitanti di città tanto antica e maravigliosa a ritirare le migliori sostante e famiglie inhabili altrove per assicurarle da ogni insulto, quando si leverà di là l' armata --- et a gl' altri si davano l'armi, che formarono un gran corpo da resistere all' incursioni de' Turchi."[10] The news of the construction of the wall caused great satisfaction at Venice, " parendo che svanisca il dubbio si era concepito che si dovesse smantellare e trasportare li abitanti in Morea."[11] The despair of the Athenians at the order to leave and their offer of 20,000 reali toward the expense of fortifying the city, as reported by Bulifon's officer and by Mateses[12] are not noticed in the *Avvisi*, but it is clear from the words of Ivanovich that some efforts were made in Venice to secure the defense of the city, though without success.

The transportation began before the reply of the Senate arrived, for at the Council of War held on February twelfth, which decided to disarm and abandon the Acropolis as well as the city, Morosini reported that the Greeks had begun to move their property to the Morea, and on February twentieth Mateses heard that three ships had been loaded for Zante and others for Coron and Nauplia.[13] The task, however, was no small one; available ships seem to have been few, and we learn from the Inquisitori that as late as March seventeenth " gl' Atheniesi facevano a furia imbarcare le loro robbe sopra vascelli destinatigli; li principali anderanno a Napoli di Romania et altri luoghi di Morea, e le genti ordinarie e che già erano armate si fermeranno a Corinto ove, allogiate le loro famiglie, disegnavano ridursi per terra per seguitare l' armata contro il nemico." [14] There was indeed good reason for haste. Sickness was rife and increasing in the army, and it was obviously imperative to move at once to more healthy quarters, yet Morosini rightly felt that it was impossible for the troops to leave until the Athenians had been placed in safety.

The presence of plague, or at any rate of fever, and its effect upon the movements of the army are passed over in silence by Ivanovich, as they are by the *Avvisi* which during the winter and early spring repeat in slightly varying forms assurances of the perfect health of the army. Quite exceptionally Rome was informed on February twenty-first that in Athens " si erano scoperte due case col mal contagioso, dicevasi introdottovi da' Turchi ad arte, ma fattesi per ordine del Signore Capitano Generale incendiare, non era passato più avanti "; [15] but this indiscretion, due to some knowledge of Morosini's letter of January sixth, was not repeated in the other letters from Venice.

Morosini's dispatches and the minutes of the Council of War tell a different story. In the late summer of 1687 the plague had appeared at various points in the Morea and this, as we have seen, had led to the decision to keep the army in Athens for the winter; but although on December seventeenth Morosini wrote in some anxiety that the plague was said to have reached Thebes, it was not until the end of the month that suspicious cases occurred among the Greeks of Athens.[16] Morosini took prompt measures, as is shown by his letter of January sixth,[17] where after mentioning a fresh outbreak at Nauplia, he continues: "A questo sinistro caso aggiontosi certo sospetto occorso in Atene di due persone morte con qualche indicio, sebene doppo d' essersi fatta di mio ordine dalla pontualità dell' Illustrissimo

Signor Proveditore Estraordinario Dolfino incendiar la casa colle due più contigue, non s' è inteso, Lode all' Altissimo, altra infausta insorgenza." As the trouble had reached Aegina and other islands, it was decided to appoint a " Magistrato alla Sanità " of three nobles with full power to take whatever measures they might deem necessary to ward off the threatened danger, and Morosini consoled himself with the consideration that though the disease had spread widely, it assumed a mild form, " onde l' influenza tiene sembianza più tosto d'una specie d'epidemica malignità in certo modo comunicativa, che di lettale pestilential contaggio." In fact while naturally anxious about the possibility of an epidemic in the army, he seems to have been chiefly troubled by the fear that these outbreaks in the Morea and elsewhere might delay the sending of reinforcements for the next campaign, just as a year earlier fear of the plague had diverted the Papal, Florentine, and Maltese contingents from his army to that of his rival Cornaro in Dalmatia.

Although Locatelli [18] asserts that by January fifth a Lazaretto had been established, and that the plague was increasing, especially among the northern troops, where the characteristic swellings were not recognized by the doctors and were treated as abscesses, it would seem that the measures taken were effective, for a long letter of Morosini, written on February twelfth, is chiefly devoted to plans for the next campaign, and merely notes that the plague in the Morea is decreasing and may be expected to end soon, " presservandosi intanto, colla protettione del Cielo, non meno l' armata di terra che di mare immune da disastri, et in una salute, che mai nei sverni passati s' è goduta "; nor do the minutes of the Council of War held on the same date [19] contain references to any epidemic in the army at Athens.

Immediately after this Council Morosini went to Nauplia

to settle the fate of the Turks of Mistra. When he returned on March fourteenth,[20] he found that the situation had changed for the worse. Dolfin reported an increase of suspicious cases and the need of special precautions against the spread of the disease. A Council of War on March fifteenth decided to continue the segregation of all doubtful cases in Athens, to hasten the departure of the Athenians, and if matters grew worse, to bring the troops down to the coast behind the recently constructed trench, which would cut off communications with the country. On March twentieth they voted that the artillery from the Acropolis and the heavy baggage should be brought down at once, so that there might be no obstacle to a prompt departure. Morosini, however, in his two letters of March eighteenth, in which he defends the decision to abandon the Acropolis as well as Athens and discusses questions of organization, does not dwell on any increased danger to the health of the army, and his letter of the nineteenth, which is chiefly occupied with the affairs of Mistra, merely reports the decision of the Council to withdraw the troops, " quando, tolga il Cielo, prendessero maggior piede i sospetti non per anco resi tali, che vagliono a stabilire di maligna infettione li accidenti occorsi. Consistono questi nello scoprirsi in alcun de' Greci e de' soldati ancora certa specie di male, che colla prontezza però de' rimedij fa che li più vadino rissanando senza pure che vi sia qualità di communicativa nè d' altre peggiori circonstanze." [21]

It is clear that in this letter Morosini endeavored to put the best face on the situation, for on the next day (March twentieth) the Council of War heard that illness was increasing and that it was more than ever necessary to separate the army from the natives. Yet Morosini feared to move the latter to the coast lest the soldiers might enter the abandoned, and probably infected, houses in search of plunder, while, as Morosini told the Council, to bring down the army first left " quei miserabili [Greci] esposti ad esser da' nemici tagliati." The Council decided that the army must be moved to Poros, which was to be completely closed to the Athenians, who could be taken to Nauplia and kept in strict quarantine until all danger had passed. A week later, on March twenty-eighth, there was worse news for the Council. The Athenians apparently had departed and the heavy baggage was ready to be brought down to be packed on the ships, except the galleys and geleazze, when Morosini learned " che hieri s' habbi pronata l' infausta crisi di 22 soldati, compreso un Alfiere,[22] caduti con segno letale, oltri 11 altri al giorno d' hoggi." This meant that there had been more deaths in a single day than in the entire month from February twenty-seventh, when the first cases from the army had entered the Lazaretto. The Council at once decided that all available ships must be used to transport the army *en masse* to Poros.

Accordingly on April fourth the army marched to the port,[23] and on the morning of the eighth [24] embarked for Poros, " conosciuto molto aggiustato il sitto per li molti seni che in se racchiude, abbondante d' acque dolci col scoglio per l' uso delle necessarie separationi colla terra ferma, per allogiarsi, et haver li provedimenti del vivere." [25] In a long letter from Poros on April fifteenth, Morosini described in detail the measures he had taken to prevent the contagion spreading, especially to the fleet. The soldiers were in general kept off the galleys, although it proved impossible to segregate the large number who had been exposed to infection. The sick were placed on small boats and towed over to the island. These measures were so far successful that only a few sailors were attacked on five of the ships used to transport the army.[26] A few cases on a galeazza and three galleys led to strenuous measures which preserved the rest of the fleet; but unfortunately through neglect of proper precautions and lack of appropriate medical treatment, especially in the German regiments,[27] the disease at one time reached such proportions that there were from 60 to 70 new cases and over 30 deaths a day. To lessen the alarm that these figures might well cause in Venice, Morosini enclosed a certificate signed by the doctors of the army, according to whom " viene concluso il male per una specie di contagione epidemica, prodotta dal perverso influsso, che di tanto tempo afflige queste parti, così per lo più colpisca ne' corpi estenuati, mal composti, e di pessimi cibi nodriti, secondo il fato per il più lo dimostra, adducendo infine per unico rimedio quello d' espeller con cordiali e sudiferi la malignità sua velenosa." This letter was read to the Senate on May eighth, and the same day Guasconi was given an excellent summary of the contents, including the opinion of the doctors, by Michele Foscarini, Savio di Settimana, doubtless in order that false rumors might not lead the Florentines to withhold their aid.[28] On the twelfth Guasconi confirmed this report of the true nature of the epidemic in a conversation with Giovanni Dolfin, brother of Morosini's Proveditor in Campo.[29]

Although the official *Avvisi* of the Inquisitori di Stato, like Ivanovich, were silent about the epidemic—indeed the issue of May eighth declared that the health of the army was good—Teglia's letters to Florence show that the truth was known and even exaggerated. Thus he wrote on May eighth, before the contents of Morosini's letter were published, that private letters confirmed the rumors that the " mal contagioso " was not only prevalent in the Morea but had also appeared in the army and even in the fleet: " Si parla di ciò a mezza voce con qualche riguardo di questa publicatione, nè io con la propria debolezza intendo d' oppormi a quello che ne possa essere scritto diversimente, umiliando le mie notitie alla censura di più accreditata penna che sia per minorare la fama di questo male, che prego Dio s' annienti del tutto, ma pur troppo dubito sia maggiore di quello viene anche scritto, dicendo alcuni che nel campo in qualche luogo ne perischano fino a 30 il giorno; altri scrivano non farsi con tutto ciò conto alcuno di questo male reso familiare nel paese dove al solito poco si stima." [30] On the same evening Teglia wrote the Abate Carlo Antonio Gondi announcing the arrival from Athens of their protégé La Rue, " fuggendo l' universal influenza d' Athene e di Morea," [31] and it was probably to him that he owed the information in his letter to Secretary Panciatichi on May twelfth: " Di dove (*i. e.* Levante) s' attendono con desiderio nuovi avvisi migliori della salute di quelle parti, nelle quali da soggetto venuto d' Atene (La Rue?) s' asserisce non trovarsi più di 4500 in circa certo di soldati, de' quali pure ne sarà, che Dio non voglia, periti molti del male che vi è tuttavia." [32]

Once safely in Poros the isolation of the sick and other measures adopted by Königsmark on Morosini's suggestion brought about a marked improvement, and on May sixth the Captain General wrote: "Apparve ben anco nel più ardente bollor della fiamma patente il miracolo di vederla ad incredibil segno ammorcata, di maniera che, se per avanti ascendava a 60 in 70 il numero de' feriti, e sopra 30 quello de' morti, non sorpassava doppo fra gl' uni e gl' altri a venti persone." The improvement had continued so rapidly that since Easter (April eighteenth) there had been no new cases and only three deaths among those still in the Lazaretto. The blow to the small army had been severe. On April eighteenth Morosini informed the Council of War that at the landing on April ninth there had been in the army 1123 sick in the Lazaretto, of whom 217 had died and 268 been discharged as out of danger; on the fleet there had been 61 cases and 25 deaths. In his letter of May sixth to the Senate he wrote: " Per le note che doppo la sudetta partenza si son tenute risultano a 574 li morti del campo, et a 52 quelli del armata di mare." No wonder that after devout thanksgivings to Divine Providence for the cessation of the disease, he continued: " Mentre dunque con si lieti raguagli posso annunciare a Vostra Serenità questo summo gaudio (Morosini had not yet heard of the death of the Doge and his own election), non so per lo contrario astenermi d' accennarle divotamente d' esser considerabile in colpo rissentito per le accadute copiose mortalità, quando al tempo che seguì lo staccamento d' Atene, s' estendeva con horrida stragge il furor del male."

This letter reached Venice on June twenty-sixth, and the *Avvisi* hastened to announce, somewhat optimistically, " la perfetta salute che godeva tanto l' armata di mare, che di terra," [33] and Teglia heard " che in sette giorni avanti non era morto alcuno di malatia, e che, lode a Dio, s' andavano recuperando gl' infermi, fra quali non si trovava manchevoli in tutto il tempo che al numero di 800 persone comprese donne, vecchi, e ragazzi, trovandosi particolarmente sani tutti gli ufficiali maggiori.[34] His next letter on June thirtieth was less certain: " Di Levante non ho che aggiungere all' accenato con l' antecedente, correndo diversa l' oppinione circa la salute di quelle parti, dove si trovano l' armata di terra e di mare, poichè le lettere del Serenissimo Capitano Generale scrisse in privato sono d' un tenore misto di speranza e di timore in questo particolare." [35] Whatever anxiety Morosini may have expressed in his private letters must have been dispelled when it became clear that the rumors of disease in the army would not prevent the arrival of the expected reinforcements, even though they were so delayed that it was not until July seventh that the expedition was at last able to leave Poros for Negroponte.[36]

APPENDIX IV

The Opposition to Morosini

The remark of the foreign ambassador, with which Ivanovich closes his account of Morosini's election, suggests that in spite of the unanimity of the electors, there was by no means universal agreement in the wisdom of their choice. The presence of this opposition is little noticed by the contemporary Venetian writers, but that in fact there existed, especially among the nobles, a considerable party bitterly hostile to the new Doge, although perforce acquiescing in his election as inevitable, is clearly set forth in the letter which Matteo del Teglia wrote on April third announcing the election and giving in his usual somewhat clumsy style an account of the state of feeling in Venice:[1]

"Quanto a nuove non vi è la più precisa della nuova creatione del successore al defunto Serenissimo Doge, caduta, come si scrisse non potere in altro soggetto seguire, nel Signor Capitano Generale Morosini, non solo a riguardo di consultare il proprio merito ma per la positura delle correnti emergenze della Republica, che ridondono in avantaggio del fortunato ascendente di Sua Eccellenza, l' esaltazione della quale non riceve altro applauso che il popolare, che non scorge con la propria debole vista oltre la scorza delle cose più rilevanti, nè altri honori che dagl' interessati parenti che gli producono a vista universale il proprio dispendio,[2] apparendo, si può dire, o livore o l' invidia ne' maggiori. In questa ellettione si può anco dire, che gl' ellettori di sua Serenità (la cui lista qui aggiunta vedrà Vostra Signoria Illustrissima[3]) habbino in questa occasione contravenuti agl' instituti e massime della Republica Serenissima, che sono d' haver per Capo un soggetto di poca testa e meno condotta, il che non può dirsi del presente, che abbonda dell'una e dell' altra. Onde le parerà forse strano il passare da un estremo all' altro, da piena autorità imperiale d' un' armata a un limitato termine, si può dir, d' obbedienza, non potendo la Serenità sua in qualità di Doge disporre del Publico più che la somma di 25 ducati senza passare per le solite ballottationi;[4] nè si può dire nè meno che habbino questi fatto alcun errore nell' ellettione predetta, perchè hanno seguitato il corso della fortuna nella positura delle cose presenti, che gl' ha posti in tale necessità, massime havendo i parenti della Serenità sua supplicati per la dignità della medesima, non poteva il broglio negarle questa sodisfazione per non disgustare un soggetto che tiene le forze in mano, e che ha spiriti sollevati da fare apparire la distintione del suo ministero con il render più e meno vantagiose l' operationi al publico servizio, senza obligo di renderne conto, benchè non si vogli credere capace d' attione veruna degenerante dal proprio debito, e di qui è che per concorrere pienamente nei sentimenti di simulata gratitudine s' è ritirato dalla pretensione ogni concorente."[5]

An important element in this opposition, if not its actual source, was what Teglia well calls "l' invidiosa emulazione fra il Proveditore Generale Cornaro e 'l Capitano Generale Morosini,"[6] which manifested itself in 1684, at the very beginning of the war, when Cornaro was at Corfu. Misled by a report that Santa Maura was weakly held by the Turks and apparently eager to gain the credit of the first victory, he hastily led his small force against the island without waiting for the arrival of Morosini with the full strength of the Venetian fleet and army, found that the Turks were on the alert, and returned to Corfu without attempting a landing.[7] Such a failure, especially when contrasted with Morosini's prompt capture of the fortress and reduction of the whole island, cannot have enhanced his reputation, and during 1685 we find him in the position of Proveditor Generale dell' Isole, an important and honorable command, but not at this time involving contact with the enemy.[8]

At the end of the year he was appointed Proveditore Generale Estraordinario in Dalmatia,[9] where the Venetian operations seem hitherto to have been somewhat desultory and ineffective. Although the forces at his disposal cannot have been large, he was able in 1686 to take Sinj, and when early in April, 1687, the Turks endeavored to recapture the town, he compelled them to raise the siege and retreat without venturing on a pitched battle. This success was promptly used by his friends in Venice as a strong argument in favor of strengthening the army in Dalmatia,[10] and when the reports of the presence of the plague in the Morea led the Maltese, Papal, and Florentine contingents to refuse to join Morosini,[11] these troops and other reinforcements from Venice were diverted to Cornaro,[12] who now felt strong enough to attack the important position of Castel Nuovo at the entrance to the Gulf of Cattaro.[13] The capture, however, proved no easy matter. The place was strongly fortified and stubbornly defended, so that the siege dragged on for some weeks to the great anxiety of Cornaro's friends, as may be seen from a long letter written by Teglia on September seventeenth. He points out how seriously failure would injure Cornaro, while the rapid successes of Morosini at Patras and Corinth have caused him to be regarded as the saviour of the country from becoming a tributary of Turkey.[14] Three days later the rivalry with Morosini appears again, when Teglia, in sending long reports of a successful assault on the Turkish forts, enlarges upon the courageous resistance of the defenders, " differente della viltà di quelli di Morea per rendere più gloriosa l' impresa." [15] Castel Nuovo finally surrendered on September thirtieth,[16] the festival of San Girolamo, the patron saint of the General, and for this victory Cornaro was rewarded with the dignity of Procuratore di San Marco Sopranumerario, the same honor that had been bestowed on Morosini in 1669 for his heroic, though unsuccessful, defence of Candia.[17] Teglia, however, in his letter of October twenty-ninth noted regretfully that in a largely attended Council there were two hundred votes against this appointment, and added the following comments on the situation as it appeared to the partisans of Cornaro, among whom he is certainly to be numbered:[18]

" Per questa creazione si può dire tutta la città in dimostrazione d' allegrezza, perchè fra congiunti ed aderanti la sua gran Casa tira grandissimo partito nella città; dico dimostrazione, perchè non tutti la fanno di cuor sincero a causa degli interessati brogli e dell' invidia, che produce livore incredibile anco fra più congiunti. Ciò poco rileva, l' honore è già conferito, ed il credito di Sua Eccellenza fortificato, di modo che se cadesse il caso di Capitano Generale, il posto sarà sicuro di questo soggetto; di qui è che non si vedrà sì facilmente il Signor Capitano Generale chiedere la permissione di ripatriare come ha fatto fin' hora ogni anno artificiosamente per rendersi più conspicuo nella stima del Senato col farsi dal medesimo pressare, vedendo di non haver successori nel posto, il che hora non segue.[19] Si vuole però, per quanto si puòle, fermare il corso alle glorie maggiori del Signore Cavaliere Cornaro che poscia nella ventura campagna proseguirà co' progressi delle vittorie nella Provincia che governa, mentre di già rimangono destinate le truppe di quella per la ventura stagione tutte in Levante, per dove solo qui si fanno le provisioni di milizie, e d' altro, e si calcola di qua il numero di 6000 bravi Alemanni, fra Svizzeri, Baraidi, e Bransvich Wolffempütel, che al fine di Marzo devon essere all' armata, sì che il Signor Cavaliere General Cornaro resterà con poca gente ozioso in

Dalmatia col savio pretesto di non impegnarsi a doppia guerra, nè tirare gl' umori alla testa con maggiore pericolo dell' infermo corpo politico." [20]

The last sentence shows that Cornaro's success had brought into question the future conduct of the war; for, with the command of the Gulf of Cattaro secured by the possession of Castel Nuovo, it might well seem that Dalmatia offered a better field for future conquest than the Levant, since it could be maintained that the extension of operations beyond the Morea would require efforts which would test severely the resources of the Republic. It is hardly surprising, therefore, to learn from Teglia's letter of November eighth that the impending departure of 1500 new troops for the seat of war had led to a sharp controversy between the partisans of Cornaro and of Morosini as to their destination and the regions in which there should be renewed military operations, or a pause.[21] These disputes seem to have continued throughout the winter, and to have aroused much feeling.[22] Nor were the generals themselves free from the suspicion of exploiting doubtful information which might influence the decisions of the government. Thus on January seventh Guasconi wrote that the Senate had been informed that the Albanians had determined to ask the protection of the Emperor, if they were not vigorously supported by the Venetian army, and that in consequence some of the Savii advocated a division of the forces in the next campaign, while others still favored giving the chief support to Morosini. In fact, he explains, many believed this reported request of the Albanians to be merely " un tratto di finezza " of Cornaro to secure the troops for himself.[23] A month later came the counter stroke. We learn from Guasconi that recent information from Morosini, alleging that the new Grand Vizier was to take command himself at Negroponte, was thought to be a similar " finezza " on his part, since Belgrade (then seriously threatened by the Imperialists) was obviously of much greater importance to the Turks than Negroponte.[24]

How far Cornaro's friends were prepared to go in their efforts to secure the diversion of important forces to Dalmatia appears from an interview which Guasconi describes in his letter of February fourteenth.[25] After speaking of the efforts of the Government to collect an army for the coming campaign, he continues: " Questa mattina essendo con il Signor Procuratore Antonio Grimani, cogniato del Signor General Cornaro, mi ha Sua Eccellenza domandato dove quest' anno andaranno le galere del Serenissimo Gran Duca, nostro Signore; al che havendo soggiunto che non era a mia notitia, ma che credevo che seguiterebbero l' esempio dell' altre squadre, mi replicò il Signor Procuratore, che stati i sospetti di Levante sperava dovessero tutte venire in Dalmatia, mostrandone una gran passione, e lasciandosi quasi intendere che a Roma se ne fusse fatto qualche progetto; il Governo però qui pare tutto intento ad accudire vigorosamente alle cose di Levante, stando sul cuore l' impresa di Negroponte, che si considera come antemurale del Regnio della Morea." As the last sentence shows, opinion in the Senate was, as usual, on the side of Morosini, and even before the death of the Doge Giustiniani a definite decision had been reached to prosecute the war with all possible energy in Greece.[26] After Morosini's election there could, of course, be no further question of weakening his army, although Cornaro was left with sufficient strength to undertake, before the summer was over, a successful attack on Knin.[27]

The question naturally arises how a proposition to withdraw support in large measure from a uniformly victorious leader could have been seriously proposed and apparently have received a certain amount of approval. Doubts about the prudence of a further advance in Greece and the ambition of a somewhat jealous rival would hardly have sufficed, had not Morosini himself on occasion provided material for criticism to his detractors. His undoubted military ability, his bold yet not reckless strategy, his tireless energy and determination were accompanied by an imperious nature, which was impatient of opposition, often rude in speech,[28] and capable at times of regrettable outbursts, even in his communications with the government.[29]

It does not appear that these defects interfered with his success in the field. His relations with Königsmark, whose experience and skill he valued highly, seem to have been always good, and even when his own wishes were directly thwarted by Königsmark's refusal to approve a sudden descent on Negroponte after the capture of Athens, his letter of October tenth to the Senate shows indeed his disappointment at this decision, but no trace of irritation with the General.[30] On the other hand he often complains bitterly in his letters of his inability to enforce his authority over the German troops, whose discipline by the terms of their engagement was wholly in the hands of their own officers,[31] and in the frequent controversies which arose from these conditions he was thought by some to have aggravated the ill-feeling by his harshness and lack of tact.[32]

The same qualities which caused friction in the army must also have militated against his popularity among his fellow nobles at home and thus have strengthened the opposition, of which he was naturally fully informed and which he resented—somewhat unreasonably, since it is certain that at no time did he lack the confidence and support of the Senate. Even after Negroponte, when a storm of abuse burst upon him, and Teglia could write: " Non si parla punto di ciò che scriva in publico per sua discolpa il Serenissimo Capitano Generale, se non che s' osservano sbigottiti li suoi parziali e affezionati, parlando gl' altri con libertà degl' errori che s' attribuiscono alla Consulta e basando la Serenità sua di testardo, altiero, avido e simili disfatti per caricarlo," even then, according to Foscarini, " il Senato prudente, e costante consolò l' afflittioni del Doge, che oltre qualche indispositione patita nel tempo dell' attacco, si trovò doppo gagliardamente oppresso nella salute, ricercandolo in viva maniera à continuare alla Patria la sua stimata direttione "; [33] and on his return to Venice in 1689, when his health would not permit him to continue longer in command, he was received in triumph. This hold upon the Senate and Great Council is hardly surprising when we read the summary of his character given by Garzoni after his death. " Fù – – – di lingua, e di letteratura bastevolmente fornito; di buon' ingegno, e d' ugualmente saldo, e pesato giudicio; grande sperienza, e conoscimento della guerra, e principalmente della professione maritima; intrepido nelle avversità, e facile al perdono. – – – morì nel maggior comando della Repubblica, e lasciò impressa un' ardente brama, che più lungamente vivesse. In molte virtù, ch' egli havea, era desiderato adorno di tutte. È provido consiglio, non colpa della natura, che non vi sia perfezione in terra. L'havrebbono voluto più blando, e mansueto; ma se cadeva in qualche muovimento d' ira, presto sedava l' animo, e riducevasi in calma." [34]

Although Ivanovich does not seem to have allowed these disputes to influence his narrative, there can be little doubt on which side his sympathies were engaged, for his earlier literary life in Venice had brought him into somewhat close connection with the related families of Grimani and Cornaro. His *drammi in musica* had been produced in the Teatro Grimani, the Venetian edition of his *Circe* (1679) dedicated to Giovanni Cornaro, and the marriage of Marino and Paolina Grimani in 1666 celebrated by an ode dedicated to Marino, "mio Patrono colendissimo."[35] Moreover even apart from such connections he had a strong motive for devotion to Cornaro, whose victories were driving the Turks from his native land, and his gratitude found expression in effusive letters and sonnets to his "adorato Padrone" after the relief of Sinj, the capture of Castel Nuovo, and the election as Procuratore Sopranumerario.[36]

Yet if he was thus naturally predisposed in favor of Cornaro, he was certainly no depreciator of Morosini, whose heroic deeds in the Cretan War he had already celebrated in his *Poesie*.[37] In fact from the capture of Santa Maura in 1684 to the occupation of Corinth in 1687 each notable triumph was marked by a congratulatory letter and sonnet, for which Morosini duly returned brief but appreciative thanks;[38] and if, in a letter to Giovanni Pesaro giving him news of the capture of both Castel Nuovo and of Athens, he rejoices especially in the liberation of his country from mohammedanism, he bestows equal praise on both victors, declaring that Cornaro has fully deserved to be made Procurator, and Morosini to receive the honor of a statue in his lifetime.[39] There are, however, some slight indications that this enthusiasm soon began to wane. Apparently neither congratulatory letter nor sonnet celebrated the capture of Athens; there is a plain suggestion that the change in Morosini's fortune was a punishment for his abandonment of the city;[40] and finally the brief and formal eulogy, which explains the almost unprecedented unanimity of the election of the Doge, is followed by the remark of the foreign ambassador,[41] which is evidently inserted to show that this unity was more apparent than real.

NOTES

NOTES TO CHAPTER I

[1] Call Number, Ott. 404. 6*. 2 vols. in 6; 4°. 24. 3 cm. by 16. 7 cm. Contemporary binding in flexible vellum. The manuscript was given to the Harvard Library by the late Professor A. C. Coolidge on June 22, 1901. It was formerly in the library of Frederick North, fifth Earl of Guilford, whose bookplate it contains, and later belonged to Sir Thomas Phillipps. The six volumes are all numbered 7366, and volumes 2, 3, 4, and 6 are also numbered 7783, 7784, 7785, and 7786, while volume 5 is marked 7366, vol. 2. The pages are numbered only in volume 1 and irregularly in Book I of volume 2.

The title-page in volume I reads: *ISTORIA Della Lega Ortodossa Contra il Turco. In tre Tomi. Contiene questo Primo La Prima Lega che fu stabilita L'anno 1683 tra La Germania e La Polonia. Tratta il secondo La Seconda ristabilita in terzo Luogo 1684 con La Republica di Venezia. Continua il Terzo con Le due sudette e La Terza Trasversale tra La Polonia e La Moscovia 1687. In ogn' uno de' quali s' inseriscono varie notizie de' Tempi dello Stato de' Collegati, dell' Emergenze più curiose dell' Europa. Di Cristoforo Ivanovich Canonico della Augusta Basilica di San Marco.* *Augusta* is written above an erased *Regia*.

Volume 1 contains *Tomo Primo*. Volumes 2 to 6 form successive parts of *Tomo Secondo*, each volume narrating in three books the events of a single year from 1684 to 1688. The plan to begin *Tomo Terzo* with 1687 was evidently abandoned, for volumes 5 and 6, from which our extracts are taken, are entitled: *Istoria Della Lega ortodossa Contra il Turco Tra la Germania, Polonia, e Venezia 1687* (or *1688*). *Tomo Secondo Campeggiamento Quarto* (or *Quinto*) *di Cristoforo Canonico Ivanovich.* The manuscript bears every evidence of being the author's fair copy. There are few erasures, but occasional marginal notes show that the work had not received its final form, and the pages for summaries at the beginning of each book are blank. The last volume is obviously unfinished (see above, p. 7).

[2] These works are:

Poesie di Cristoforo Ivanovich. Con l'aggiunta di varie Lettere di Proposta, e Risposta, e della Fenice Panegirico alla memoria del gran Lazzero Mocenigo. Venezia, 1675. The work is dedicated to Ranuccio II Farnese, Duke of Parma.

Minerva al Tavolino. Lettere diverse di Proposta, e Risposta à varii Personaggi, sparse d' alcuni componimenti in Prosa ed in Verso:

Con Memorie Teatrali di Venezia. Di Cristoforo Ivanovich, Canonico della Basilica Ducale. Parte Prima. Venezia, 1681. (*Seconda Impressione*, 1688). *Parte Seconda.* Venezia, 1688. This volume adds to the title after *Verso, Concernenti per lo più alle Vittorie della Lega contra il Turco sino questo Anno*; and naturally omits *Con Memorie Teatrali di Venezia*. The first part is dedicated to the three sons of Ranuccio II, and the second to Prince Ferdinand of Tuscany, eldest son of the Grand Duke, Cosimo III, who visited Venice late in 1687, while this volume was passing through the press. Part I contains (pp. 140-145) a lengthy and highly eulogistic recommendation of Ivanovich to Prince Carlo of Carrara by Dom Antonio Lupis, with a brief account of his life. The recommendation is not dated, but Ivanovich's letter of thanks to Lupis was written on May 2, 1678.

See also: Giustiniano Martinioni, *Primo Catalogo de gl' Huomini Letterati Veneti*, p. 2, in his *Aggiunta* to Sansovino, *Venetia, Città nobilissima et singolare* (Venezia, 1663); Gregorio Leti, *L'Italia Regnante* (Geneva, 1676), vol. IV, parte IV, libro I, pp. 219-222; brief notices in F. S. Quadri, *Della storia e della ragione d' ogni Poesia* (Bologna, Milano, 1739-1751), vol. II, p. 330, and vol. V, pp. 426, 473.

[3] The date of his birth is known only from the inscription on his tomb in the church of San Moisè in Venice, which gives his age as sixty at his death in 1688 (see below, Chap. I, note 30). The inscription around his portrait in the *Poesie* (1675)—CHRISTOPHORUS IVANOVICH EPIROTA NOBILIS BUDUENSIS I. U. D. AET. ANN. XLIV—can hardly be used as evidence for his birth in 1631, for it is repeated without change in *Minerva*, I (1681).

In reply to an inquiry whether his family was connected with a family of the same name which appeared in early Russian history, he wrote from Venice on November 6, 1683: " Della notizia poi della mia discendenza in ordine al fondamento dell' Istorie di Moscavia, non sò dirle altro, se non, che sono à mano trè secoli, dà che la mia famiglia riconosce la Nobiltà in Albania, ed è dal tempo appunto, che il Turco spogliò Georgio Despoto del Regno di Servia, e Bulgaria, restando trà le altre famiglie Nobili anco questa mia sotto l' Augusto Dominio della Serenissima Republica " (*Minerva*, II, p. 186). His coat of arms appears below the portrait in the *Poesie* and *Minerva*, I, as well as on his tomb. He describes it as " un Rovere, intorno al cui tronco stà attorcigliato un' Angue, dalla cui bocca esce un Fanciullo ignudo " (*Minerva*, II, p. 396). It thus bears a curious resemblance to a combination of the well-known arms of the Rovere and Sforza.

[4] " Profittava egli molto ne' studij, quando mossa la guerra da Ibraimo a' Veneziani pensò di partire dalla Patria, come posta all' ultimo confin del Barbaro, così esposta à continue molestie, e pericoli e di portarsi in Italia " (Lupis, *Minerva*, I, p. 141).

[5] *Poesie*, Preface; cited also by Leti, *Italia Regnante*, IV, p. 222.

[6] The date of his departure is uncertain. It would be natural to suppose that he took advantage of the only recorded appearance of the Venetian fleet at Budua in 1649 to leave the country, but I have found no evidence of his presence in Italy before 1654, and it is perhaps significant that in this year we hear that small armed Turkish vessels had begun to harass trade in the Adriatic. On this phase of the war see G. Brusoni, *Historia dell' ultima guerra trà Veneziani e Turchi* (Venezia, 1673), pp. 224 ff. and 254.

[7] *Poesie*, Preface: " Benchè sia il mio nativo idioma tutto diverso dal Toscano, la Fortuna, che mi portò in Italia, à cagione della passata Guerra col Turco, mi fece attento all' Accademie più fiorite, e nell' ore oziose, all' esercizio della mia debole Musa." To the end of his life he was anxious about the purity of his style, and in the Preface to *Minerva*, II, addressed " Al Dotto Lettore," he writes: " L'Idioma è Toscano acquistato da me più con lo studio, che con la pratica. Se non ti riuscirà sovravolgere, incolperai il Destino, che mi fè nascere Forestiero, più frà l' armi, che frà le lettere."

[8] Ivanovich wrote to Paolo Adriani at Verona, October 29, 1675: " [Verona] una Città, che porto scolpita nel più vivo dell' anima - - -. Già negli anni più verdi sbalzato da una disastrosa fortuna, che raggirava la mia Patria frà le stragi della passata guerra col Turco, mi accolse Verona. In un triennio del mio soggiorno hò contratto debiti immensi di gratitudine, perchè non hò trascorso giornata, in cui non abbia veduto assollarmisi intorno le grazie ed i favori - - -. Mi sortì l' anno 1654 di vedere una giostra nobilissima, - - - in quel superbissimo Anfiteatro " (*Minerva*, I, pp. 69-70). " L' accolse Verona, e coll' Accademie sue l' allettò maggiormente alle virtù, e specialmente alla Poesia - - -. Dall' Accademia Filarmonica (*i. e.* Verona) passò alla Delfica (*i. e.* Venice)" (Lupis, *ibid.*, p. 141). Ivanovich was evidently proud of his membership in these Academies, for they are represented on his tomb; the Filarmonica by a Siren holding an astrolabe, with the inscription, *Caelorum imitatur concentum*; the Delfica by a tripod, and the inscription, *Huic oracula*.

[9] The *Poesie*, pp. 309 ff., contains letters from Verona dated 15 Maggio, 1656, and 25 Febraro, 1657 (Ivanovich seems to use gen-

erally the New Style in dating his letters) ; but the prefatory note to his poem, *Il Trionfo Navale à Dardanelli*, is dated " Venezia, il 1 Aprile, 1657 " (*Poesie*, p. 192).

[10] In 1649 Leonardo Pesaro, " Nepote di Giovanni Pesaro Doge," was one of the Venetian gentlemen who bought the title of Procurator of San Marco for 20,000 ducats or more (Martinioni, *Aggiunta* to Sansovino, *Venetia*, p. 725). Giovanni Pisano was Doge in 1658-1659.

[11] For these poems see the Indices in E. A. Cicogna, *Saggio di Bibliografia Veneziana* (Venezia, 1847) ; G. Soranzo, *Bibliografia Veneziana* (Venezia, 1884-1885) ; A. Medin, *Storia della Republica di Venezia nella poesia* (Milano, 1904).

[12] Martinioni in the *Catalogo*, p. 2: " Christoforo Ivanovich, nato in Epiro, di dove portatosi in Venetia à causa della presente guerra col Turco, si trattene per segretario di Lettere appresso Leonardo Pesaro Procurator di S. Marco. Egualmente riguardevole in Verso, ed in Prosa si è resa la sua virtu."

[13] The silence of Martinioni probably indicates that he had not received the degree in 1663. The inscription on his portrait shows that he had obtained it by 1672, and in 1678 Lupis (*Minerva*, I, p. 142), after quoting Martinioni, continues " aggiunse a' Lauri Poetici la laurea in ambe le leggi."

[14] For the titles see G. Leti, *L' Italia Regnante*, IV, pp. 220-221.

[15] *La Veneta Costanza nel famoso triennio di Candia* (also in *Poesie*, pp. 241 ff.).

[16] *Poesie*, Preface, cited by Leti, *L' Italia Regnante*, IV, p. 222.

[17] On the general character of the poems inspired by the great deeds of the Cretan War, Medin, *op. cit.*, p. 318: " L' antitesi tra la grandezza dell' impresa e la miseria pur talvolta tanto pretensiosa di quei versi è così stridente, che deploriamo la sorte toccata agli eroi di Candia di essere caduti, anche dopo morte, in mani assai spesso non meno sacrileghe di quelle dei loro carnefici." On the heroic death of Lorenzo Marcello in the victory at the Dardanelles, *ibid.*, p. 331: " Non una delle poche poesie italiane che conosciamo è immeritevole dell' oblio in cui è caduta ; - - - lo stesso poemetto dell' Ivanovich è una delle solite rifritture epiche, con lo scopo, non tanto di narrare il fatto, quanto di prendere pretesto da quello per ricalcare la *Gerusalemme Liberata* e altri modelli ben noti, ripetendo i soliti luoghi comuni abusati in siffatto genere ibrido e falso di poesia. Sono cento ottave, e non una, neppure là ove si accenna alla morte del Marcello, vale a sollevarci dalla noia di questo poemetto freddo e monotono." On the

three years' defence of Candia, *ibid.*, pp. 341-342: " Cristoforo Ivanovich, non contento dei suoi versi infelicissimi per la battaglia dei Dardanelli, compose un poemetto *eroico* di tre canti in versi sciolti sul ' famoso triennio '; ma, al solito, in luogo di chiedere ispirazione ai fatti già di per se tanto poetici, si mostra tutto intento a non scostarsi dai noti modelli e quindi ad abbellire gli episodi storici con le usate finzioni, con gli arzigogoli e con le sottigliezze e iperboli più strampalate - - -. Naturalmente, in un poemetto di tre canti, com' è quello dell' Ivanovich, non manca qualche generosa invocazione, qualche nobile pensiero, ma sono pur sempre rare eccezioni; e se, ad esempio, il poeta, che poi non era dei peggiori del tempo suo, si giova di una iperbole non inefficace dicendo che il valore dei Veneziani ' ha portato spavento anche alla Morte ' ei però l'aveva di già guastata coi versi che immediatamente la precedono."

Even more severe is the judgment of P. Selvatico and V. Lazari, *Guida di Venezia e delle isole circonvicine* (Venezia, 1852), p. 74, *Nota storica* on the monument in S. Moisè: " L' Ivanovich fu onesto canonico di S. Marco e scellerato poeta. I suoi versi sono più spaventevoli del suo mausoleo. Il che non è poco."

[18] Lupis (*Minerva*, I, p. 143): " Leonardo Pesaro Procurator di San Marco sudetto destinato dalla Republica uno de' quattro Ambasciatori di congratulazione al nuovo Pontifice Innocenzio Undecimo, lo fece suo Mastro di Camera." On February 10, 1676, Lupis wrote to Ivanovich (*ibid.,* p. 137); " Con esser stata graduata V. S. Reverendissima all' Insigne Zanfarda della Chiesa Ducale di S. Marco, hà riscosso un giustissimo tributo al suo merito." On February 13, Padre Abate Giudici also congratulated him (*ibid.*, p. 133): " La carica poi di Mastro di Camera destinatale nell' Ambasciata di Roma, si conveniva al merito ed alle condizioni del mio caro Signor D. Cristoforo - - - . La Zanfarda, che S. Eccellenza hà voluto conferirle nella Basilica Ducale di S. Marco, e la presente carica, sono indicij di quelle fortune, che può ottenerle un mezzo così cospicuo, ed osservabile presso il Papa." It does not appear, however, that this visit to Rome brought Ivanovich any recognition from the Pope.

The zanfarda is defined by F. Mutinelli as " gufo, o pellicia, usata dai canonici, e dai sottocanonici della cattedrale di S. Pietro di Castello, e della ducale basilica di S. Marco, portata sul braccio sinistro per distintivo del loro grado " (*Lessico Veneto,* Venezia, 1852, *s. v.* Almutia). That the zanfarda in this case was conferred on a *sottocanonico* is certain, for Ivanovich was promoted to canon in 1681.

[19] Lupis (*Minerva*, I, p. 143) writes in 1678: " Al presente risiede zanfardato in Canonica Ducale."

[20] In reply to a letter of congratulation on this preferment, Ivanovich refers to " il Canonicato conferitomi dalla Clemenza di queste Principe Serenissimo Luigi Contarini " (*Minerva*, II, p. 76).

[21] *Minerva*, II, pp. 99-116.

[22] *Minerva*, I, pp. 366 ff. F. S. Quadri, *op. cit.*, V, p. 426.

[23] See below Appendix IV, notes 36-38.

[24] See note 2, above.

[25] See e. g. note 18, above.

[26] Lupis, *Minerva*, I, pp. 143 f.

[27] Nicolò Coleti, *Monumenta Ecclesiae Venetae Sancti Moysis,* (Venetia, 1758), pp. 261-262: " Novimus praeterea ex praedictis Actis Capitularibus, Christophorum Ivanovich Ducalis basilicae Canonicum obtinuisse in Ecclesia nostra locum, ubi monumentum atque sepulcrum sibi extruenda curaret. Primo namque Christophoro exposcenti spatium illud interioris parietis, quod supra lateralem imi templi januam, turrique propiorem, adusque fenestram protenditur pro inibi monumento construendo, et e regione ipsius januae in pavimento eum locum, qui sibi soli parando sepulcro sufficeret, offerentique propterea octoginta ducatorum eleemosynam, annuit Ecclesiae Collegium die 8 Decembris anni 1680, capitulariter congregatum. Mutata deinde sententia idem Christophorus die 24 Septembris anni 1684 supplici libello, novaque oblata quinquaginta ducatorum eleemosyna, rogavit, ut duplex locus sibi quadriennio ante concessus, et Ecclesiae juri mox restituendus, geminis aliis opposti Ecclesiae lateris permutaretur, eo nempe quo paries interior a suprema lateralis januae parte ad templi coronam inter extantes utrinque pilas excurrit, et consequenter eidem e dictae januae regione subjecto pavimento. Novis hisce Christophori votis eodem die itidem acquievit Ecclesiae Collegium: ac brevi emersit nobilissimum illud, ac inter caetera Ecclesiae nostrae opera spectatissimum monumentum, de quo, non secus ac de Christophori sepulcro, verba faciendi alibi occurret occasio." The promised description of the monument is on page 336.

Ivanovich clearly took great pride in his monument, of which he gives an elaborate description in a long letter, written on January 20, 1684/5, to P. Giacomo Lubrani of Naples (*Minerva*, II, pp. 393-397). This description was later published with minor changes and additions to accompany an engraving by Agniello Porbio of Naples under the title *Dilucidazione del Deposito Ivanovich in S. Moisè di Venezia, s. a.*, pp. 4, 4°, with plate in folio. See Cicogna, *Bibliografia Veneziana*, p. 643, No. 4731.

[28] On the slab of red marble in the pavement below the monument are carved his coat of arms and the inscription "Conscius mortis, nescius horae, ne praeveniatur, praevenit hanc urnam suo cineri parando, Christophorus Ivanovich, I. V. D. Divi Marci Canonicus MDCLXXXIV." The monument is inscribed "Divinorum in se beneficiorum Custos, Temporis, ac Mortis Vindex, Aeternitatis Memor, non sibi, sed Deo, Vivens, Christophorus Ivanovich." At the bottom of the monument is the date MDCLXXXVIII. AET. LX.

[29] Coleti, *op. cit.*, pp. 262-263: " Praefatus deinde Christophorus Ivanovich Canonicus Ducalis, cum suam postremam voluntatem die 30 Octobris anni 1688, declarasset in actis Dominici Garzoni Paulini tabellionis Veneti, vulgatam postea ob Christophori decessum die 6 Januarii 1689, suis haeredibus mandavit, ut Sodalitii SS. Sacramenti in S. Moysis Ecclesia instituti nomine residuum quoddam occuparent. Si sors occupata, Testator inquit, viginti quatuor ducatos annuos reddiderit, Sodalitii Custos Ecclesiae Collegio singulis annis tribuet sena ducata, ut annuum funebre sacrum pro pluribus menti meae accommodandum Novembri mense solemniter peragat: quina ducata impendet in gemina funalia sepulcro meo quotannis apponenda in annua omnium fidelium defunctorum Commemoratione: terna diligenti et perito viro monumentum meum atque sarcophagum singulis cuiuslibet anni aestatibus elueti persolvet: reliqua in Sodalitii beneficium vertet. Sin plus reddiderit sors, quidquid vigintiquatuor ducatos excesserit, anniversario Defunctorum die in paroeciae pauperes erogabit. Si autem minus, pro exactae pecuniae ratione metietur expensas, et si opus fuerit, anniversarium sacrum omittet, cum statutum praefixumque mihi sit, ut Sodalitium quomodolibet annuum sex saltem ducatorum beneficium percipiat, et monumentum meum, in Ecclesiae decus et honorem Dei, nitidum servetur."

[30] Since the Venetian year began on March 1, his death in January is not in contradiction with the date on the monument.

[31] In his preface to the second volume of the *Minerva* (1688), addressed "Al Dotto Lettore," he calls attention to the fact that these letters are for the most part devoted " alle Vittorie della Lega Christiana, avute contra il Turco, l' Istoria delle quali mi stà sotto la Penna, per comparirti un giorno in abito di publica Felicità, che si và sempre più avanzando ne' Trionfi." At the end of the list of his publications in the same volume he announces as in preparation *L' Istoria della Lega Ortodossa contra il Turco, dall' Assedio di Vienna in successivi Campeggiamenti.*

[32] See, for example, above pp. 9, 12, 15, 20, 24.

NOTES TO CHAPTER II

[1] Manuscript, vol. V, lib. iii. See above, Chap. I, note 1.

[2] This decision was not reached without much discussion. At a Council of War held on August 12, immediately after the occupation of Corinth, Morosini recommended bringing the fleet without delay into the Saronic Gulf. Even if it should prove unwise to attack Negroponte at once, it would be advantageous to capture Athens, " luogo aggiustato al ricovro et alla concia dell' Armata medesima nel prossimo verno, havendo a tiro di canone Porto Draco (Piraeus) e quello molto più grande nell' Isola contigue di Caluri (Salamis)." Moreover, from this position it would be easy to levy contributions in the Archipelago, as had been done in the previous year. The Council approved and Morosini reported the decision to the Senate in his letter of August 19. He was still of the same mind when he again arrived at Corinth a month later, for at the Council of War on September 14 he urged that, although Negroponte was now too strongly fortified to be attacked successfully with the force available, it would be best to go to Athens, especially in view of the request for protection made by " quatro Primati Greci Ateniesi dalla loro Comunità inviati."

Further reflexion led him to change his mind, as is shown by the minutes of the Council of War on September 17, and his letter to the Senate on September 20 (Laborde, pp. 122-131, note). He now foresaw great difficulty in feeding the army at Athens, while its occupation would in no way protect the Isthmus against Turkish raids, and concluded " non so per alcun riguardo conoscere fruttuosa, nè opportuna l' impresa d' Atene, per dover immediatamente poi abbandonar, e distrugger, il luogo medesimo coll' esterminio di quei poveri Greci e colla perdita di nove mila reali, che annualmente corrispondono alla publica cassa " (Laborde, p. 123, note). The Council agreed that it would be best to quarter the army in the Morea for the winter, but decided before doing so to go to Athens and try to extort a contribution of 50,000 to 60,000 reali, and only if this attempt failed, to attack the city, " a fine di levare quel ricovro a' nemici, come sarebbe desiderabile poter loro distrugger parimente ogni altro confinante alloggio della Rumelia, per allontanarli di qua " (Laborde, p. 125, note). These misgivings, however, were apparently not allowed to reach the Venetian public. They are not mentioned, as is natural,

NOTES TO CHAPTER II

in the *Avvisi* issued by the Inquisitori di Stato, nor in the news-letters and pamphlets devoted to the Venetian victories. Nor is there any hint of their existence in the unofficial gossip—not always favorable to Morosini—sent to Florence by Matteo del Teglia and Alessandro Guasconi.

[3] Locatelli, II, p. 3, gives the strength of the army as 9880 infantry and 871 cavalry; Fanelli, *Atene Attica*, p. 308, as 8800 and 870 respectively; Morosini and the *Avvisi* are silent. The figures given by Ivanovich are supported by the minutes of the Council of War on November 22, 1687. Morosini then reported that Königsmark was much troubled at the recall of three veteran Brunswick regiments, numbering 1397 men, as this would leave him only 6352 " soldati sani " or, deducting officers' servants, musicians and others on special service, only 5072 available to mount guard and repel Turkish raids. As the losses in the siege of the Acropolis had been insignificant, and the general health of the army at this time was good, these figures suggest a strength on landing of something over 7749 (6352 + 1397) men. The army can hardly have lost 2000 men in two months. It is true that probably 9000 men had sailed from Santa Maura in July (*A. J. A.*, XXXVIII, 1934, p. 62, note 2) and reinforcements had later arrived, but August in Corinth had proved very unhealthy (Hombergk in Laborde, p. 354), and according to Foscarini, p. 331, the newcomers had been detailed for garrison duties in the Morea. Moreover the Council of War had voted on September 17 (Laborde, p. 125, note) that only the " militia sana " should be embarked for Athens, a vote which suggests a considerable sick list at Corinth.

[4] This was not Morosini's first visit to the Piraeus. Thirty-three years before, during the Cretan war, he had led a successful raid upon the ships in the harbor, as appears from the following letter to the Doge for the Senate:

SERENISSIME PRINCIPE.

Nel passar, che si fece li X stante alle parti di Egena fui io spedito con cinque Galere al corso delle circovicine riviere di terra ferma, e conferitomi a Porto Lione presi nove Fregadoni di molta portata, et un' altro affondato, quali s' allestivano per trasferirsi in Canea con viveri, et incendiati il giorno doppo tre altri, che sono in tutti 13 con molto Legname, con cui si doveva perfezionare la lor fabrica, e seguì ogni cosa felicemente vicin alla Città d' Athene, non ostante qualche difesa de' Turchi; così Dio Signore anco nell' evento presente dia modo di poter azzardar mia vita, con sola mira d' apportar sollievo all' Eccellenze Vostre a quali prometto, che l' Armi di questo Legno per ciò faran sempre con favore impiegate, etc.

   Di Galera Sdile li 27 Maggio 1654

                Francesco Morosini Proveditor dell' Armata.

The manuscript from which this letter is taken is in Venice, Civico Museo Correr, Archivio Morosini-Grimani, 478 (Colloc. 430): *Le Azzioni di Francesco Morosini, Principe di Venezia*, Parte Prima, p. 63. This anonymous life of Morosini, in two sumptuous volumes, was compiled in 1694, and dedicated to the nephews of the late Doge in the hope of inducing them to imitate the glorious actions of their uncle. It is almost wholly composed of his letters to the Senate. The section on Athens is in the second volume, pp. 228-232. It contains only the first part of the letter to the Senate (Laborde, pp. 157-160, note), ending with the number of the Turks who left the Acropolis. There is another copy, much less magnificent, in the Biblioteca Quirini-Stampalia, Cl. IV, 97, 98. So far as I know, this life has never been printed.

[5] The passage enclosed in brackets is written in the margin and marked for insertion at this point. It is copied, with considerable omissions, from Coronelli, *Memorie istoriografiche del Regno della Morea racquistato dall' Armi della Serenissima Republica di Venezia*, etc. (Venezia, 1688), pp. 200-202, who in turn derived his information from Spon. Unfortunately Ivanovich, in his zeal for condensation, failed to notice that the words, " Di qui dicono - - - Androgeo," referred to Porto Falero, not to Porto Lione.

[6] In placing the arrival at Piraeus and the advance of the army to Athens on successive days Ivanovich is in agreement with the *Avviso* of November 8 (Lambros, N. E., XX, 1926, p. 210; cf. the almost identical letter in Rome, Vitt. Eman., 755), which was very probably his source, and at variance apparently with all other contemporary authorities, according to whom these events occurred on the same day. The authority of Morosini (Laborde, p. 157, note) is decisive for the arrival on the morning of the twenty-first, while in view of the energy of both Morosini and Königsmark and the absence of any opposition it seems improbable that the army waited at the harbor until the evening of the following day. The only other source for the advance on the twenty-second is the *Relatione Marciana*, which how-

ever says that the army sailed from Corinth on the evening of the twenty-first: "La notte delli 21 caduto partissimo da Corinto, et la mattina sussequente arrivassimo nel porto di Atene, dove affondate l' ancore si diede principio al disbarco di tutta la militia, che seguì nel termine di due hore. Distribuito poscia l' ordine della marchia s' incaminassimo a vista della Città non più di sei miglia distante dal porto" (Lambros, Δελτίον, V, 1896-1900, p. 222). The halt for the night in the olive grove is mentioned in this *Relatione* and by Muazzo (Lambros, *loc. cit.*; Laborde, pp. 145, note, and 143, note).

[7] "Il detto giorno" is written above "alli 23," which has been crossed out.

[8] The first bomb is said to have been fired about noon on the twenty-fourth (*Z. bild. K.*, XXII, 1887, p. 369), but it was not until the next day that the batteries came into full operation (*ibid.*, p. 370). The cannon succeeded in silencing the Turkish battery in front of the Propylaea and compelled the defenders to move their guns to another part of the Acropolis: " La batteria de' canoni fece l' effetto, che si pretendeva, mentre levò le difese all' inimico, che con una batteria d' altretanti pezzi di canone andava incommodando li nostri. Fu perciò obligato a levarla, e piantarla in altro posto, e in tanto dalla parte de' nostri canoni incominciò a giocare con la moschetaria, che però non fece danno di consideratione" (*Rel. Marc.,* Lambros, Δελτίον, p. 223; omitted by Laborde. Cf. *Z. bild. K.*, *loc. cit.*, p. 369; *Avviso,* Laborde, p. 147, note).

[9] So far as I know, Ivanovich alone attributes to Morosini the command to direct the fire upon the Parthenon. Like the preceding statement that the Captain General came up from the fleet so that he might give closer supervision to the operations—a direct participation nowhere claimed by Morosini himself, who gives the credit for the successful ordering of the attack to " la versata sperienza dell' eminentissimo signor generale Konismarch " (Laborde, p. 158, note)—this order may have no better authority than the wish to magnify the importance of the Captain General. On the other hand it must be admitted that it is in no way inconsistent with his stern and ruthless methods of carrying on the war. Sobiewolsky, the authority for the deserter who brought the news that the powder magazine was in the Parthenon, does not say who gave the order to bombard the temple (Michaelis, *Der Parthenon,* Leipzig, 1871, p. 346, no. 18).

[10] This explanation of the ineffective bombardment is unique, but

may well be correct, for San Felice had a certain reputation as an inventor of new bombs (see below, note 17). Except in the official dispatches, which say little about it, the early failure is ascribed to his incompetence and even the ultimate success to luck; *e. g.* "con fortunato colpo" (Morosini, Laborde, p. 158, note); "casualmente penetrò una bomba" (Muazzo, *ibid.*, p. 143, note); "una bomba gettata a capriccio e senza regola" (*Rel. Marc., ibid.*, p. 145, note); "caduta a caso" (letter in Bulifon, *ibid.*, p. 188, note). Sobiewolsky, as is well known, attributes the hit to a Lüneburg lieutenant, while Matteo del Teglia wrote to Florence on November 8, giving the credit for the outcome, but not expressly for the successful shot, to his young favorite, La Rue: "La sorte di questo attacco toccò al Signore Rinaldo Buchett, o di vero La Rue, piantando esso la prima e la seconda batteria di commissione del suo Prefato (*sic?*) Conte di San Felice, che gli sortì felicemente, doppo alquanti tiri a vuoto; per lo che ne riportò la gloria meritata (Arch. Med., 3043, fol. 1733v). La Rue, who had come to Venice, under the assumed name of Bouchet, in 1684 as a protégé of Cosimo III, was serving as a volunteer under San Felice at the latter's request (*ibid.*, fol. 1285, March 26, 1687).

[11] This story of the destruction of the harem of the Aga by a second bomb, also fired as the result of special information, is found only here, and inevitably suggests that it is merely a variant version of the destruction of the Parthenon. We know that the Turks had brought into the temple their women, children and valuables, as well as a certain quantity of munitions and other supplies (Muazzo, Laborde, p. 143, note; Sobiewolsky, *loc. cit.*), and doubtless the Aga had transferred his harem thither from the low rooms near the ruined Propylaea where Spon had found it in 1676 (*Voyage d' Italie, de Dalmatie, de Grèce, et du Levant,* Lyon, 1678, II, p. 141). Moreover while Morosini's dispatch of October 10 (Laborde, p. 157, note; the date is fixed by the copy in the Civico Museo), the *Avviso* of November 8 (*ibid.*, p. 147, note), and the other accounts all dwell on the great explosion of September 26, which wrecked the temple and caused a fire that raged for two days among the houses that crowded the Acropolis, there is no mention of the terrible loss of life until after the occupation by the Venetians. In his letter of October 11 Morosini first refers to " più di trecento periti di sesso diverso dalla sola prodigiosa bomba che causò la desolazione del maestoso tempio dedicato a Minerva" (Laborde, p. 162, note); but this slaughter was not made public in Venice until early December, when the number of killed was

reduced to 200 (*Avviso,* Dec. 6, Laborde, p. 176, note; cf. a similar letter from Athens, dated October 27, sent to Florence by Guasconi on December 3, Arch. Med., 1577, No. 214 encl.). It seems to me probable, therefore, that the duplication of destructive bombs in our narrative is due to a failure to recognize that two accounts of the disaster caused by the " prodigiosa bomba," one of which emphasized the explosion of the munitions and the ruin of the Parthenon, while the other dwelt on the loss of life, really referred to the same event. It should be added that the *Ragguaglio giornaliero* (Omont, *R. ét. gr.,* VIII, 1895, p. 258) places the explosion of the munitions on the twenty-sixth, but mentions on the twenty-eighth, immediately before the surrender, a fresh outbreak of fire due to the continued bombardment and especially destructive of the houses. I have not found the source of Laborde's statement (p. 149) that on the evening of the twenty-fifth a bomb caused the explosion of a small magazine in the Propylaea.

[12] On Turenne see above, Appendix I, pp. 29-31.

[13] Morosini himself was very reluctant to accept anything but an unconditional surrender, and in his own words yielded " mal volentieri " to the opinion of Königsmark, who urged the natural strength of the fortress and the necessity for its speedy reduction (Laborde, p. 159, note). This reluctance dictated the fourth article of the terms of surrender, omitted in Morosini's letter, which ran " Che in caso fosse al presente la Fortezza in stretta scarsezza d' acqua, di munitioni da guerra, ò di provisioni da bocca, non habbino ad haver effetto le presenti Capitolationi, mà s' intendino ritrattate, e correr debba la resa à discrettione " (*Ragguaglio giornaliero,* said to be translated from the Turkish terms of surrender; *R. ét. gr.,* VIII, 1895, p. 259). The transport required six vessels; one English, two French, and three Ragusan (Morosini, Laborde, p. 159, note).

[14] In this passage the words in italics are interlined in the original, and those in brackets are inserted in the margin.

Morosini's own account of this visit to the city in his letter of October 10 is omitted by Laborde, but may be found in the edition of Varola and Volpato, p. 11. He says that he went up to consult Königsmark about an immediate attack on Negroponte, as the Council of War was unwilling to come to a decision without knowing the General's opinion. Accordingly " cadde in me nel proposito stesso l' incarico d' averne seco speciale discorso. Al quale effetto portatomi, sotto apparente pretesto di riveder il campo, alle sue tende." He adds an account of his interview with Königsmark who, to Morosini's great disappointment, was strongly opposed to any attempt on Negroponte, but quite ready to remain in Athens for the winter.

[15] Ivanovich apparently obtained the date of October 3 by adding five days to September 28, as he found no date in his *Avvisi*, but in fact the interval seems to have been reckoned from the twenty-ninth, for in the minutes of the Council of War held on October 2 we read of the " presidio che occorresse introdur in fortezza subito che vi saran posdimani (*i. e.* Oct. 4) usciti i Turchi " (Laborde, p. 170, note). This is also the date given by the Swedish officer in a Hanoverian regiment (*Z. bild. K.*, XXII, 1887, p. 371) and confirmed by Morosini's own statement that the Turks embarked on October 5 (Laborde, p. 159, note). The numbers in Ivanovich agree with those given by Morosini except that according to the latter there were only 500 soldiers. The little pamphlet, *Vera e Distinta Relatione dell' Acquisto della Città e Fortezza d' Athene*, etc. (Venetia, 1687), which Ivanovich almost certainly used, says " circa tre mille, e tra questi cinque in sei cento huomini d' armi."

The unfortunate refugees were not well received in Smyrna, if we can believe the *Avviso* of the Inquisitori for January 24, 1687/8: " Il capitano della sudetta nave S. Spiridione (which had just arrived at Venice) fu uno di quelli, che condusse li Turchi usciti da Athene in Smirne, dove quegli habitanti li riceverono molto mal volentieri e dissero al detto capitano, che haverebbe fatto meglio d' annegarli per viaggio mentre ivi non haverebbero fatto altro che accrescergli la carestia."

[16] This list of Venetian worthies, with merely minor verbal differences in the eulogies, is found in an *Avviso*, dated November 8, 1687, of which two copies were sent to Florence by Teglia (Misc. Med., 667; Arch. Med., 3043, fols. 1739-1740), and also in the printed *Vera e Distinta Relatione*. It seems certain that Ivanovich had either the *Avviso* or the pamphlet before him. The *Avviso* of the same date issued by the Inquisitori is wholly different (Lambros, N. E., XX, 1926, pp. 210-214; Laborde, pp. 146-148, note, from a copy dated November 22). Morosini in his letter of October 10 praises especially Dolfin, Benzon, and the five nobles, but is silent about the others.

[17] Antonio Mutoni, Conte di San Felice, of Verona, having been banished from his native city for some youthful offences, went to France, where he devoted himself to the study of mathematics,

especially ballistics, and the construction of fireworks with such success that he was employed by the King, and acquired considerable reputation. During the winter of 1685-86 he was engaged by the Venetians to command the "bombisti" and to exploit his newly invented bombs and mortars, a quantity of which were at once ordered (Foscarini, p. 259). The letters and *Avvisi* sent to Florence by Teglia in February and March, 1686, refer frequently to experiments with the new bombs, which do not seem to have proved wholly satisfactory. In fact by the middle of April there were rumors that all the heavy expenditure on the new material had been wasted, and there was much criticism of the action of the government in placing such large orders before conclusive tests had been made (Arch. Med., 3043, *e. g.* fols. 606v, 648v, 662v). Nor did the new mortars and their inventor prove more successful in the following campaign. Both at Navarino Nuovo and at Modon there were charges of incompetence (Laborde, p. 142, note; Beregani, II, p. 12; Foscarini, p. 265; Garzoni, p. 157), and that the same complaints were loud at Athens, though carefully suppressed in the official reports which were followed by Ivanovich, may be seen from the passages cited by Laborde, pp. 142, 143, 145, notes. In the last quotation from the *Relatione Marciana* the manuscript, after recounting the reprimand of Königsmark, continues with a passage omitted in large part by Laborde: "Ritornò il Mottoni al travaglio, ma nè meno gli sortì di far alcun bel colpo; onde si replicorono li rimproveri contro lo stesso dal violente irrasibile di Sua Eccellenza (*i. e.* Königsmark) a segno, che hoggidì è ridotto il ludibrio di tutta quest' armata, nè so se più potrà rimetersi in concetto. Ha però buoni Patroni appresso il Capitano Generale, onde quando Sua Eccellenza (*i. e.* Morosini) voglia protegerlo continuerà nel servitio, benchè sia di danno considerabile al Publico. Il Chinismarch gli levò la sopraintendenza ai mortari con sostituirli un altro bombista (Muazzo's 'governatore Leandro') ma nel punto ch' era per farne la consegna, una bomba - - - andò a cadere sul tempio di Pallade - - -. Onde l' Eccellentissimo Dolfin Proveditor in Campo si fece mediatore appresso il Chinismarch, acciò gli restituisse la sopraintendenza, conforme fecce." (*Rel. Marc.*, fol. 103; Lambros, $\Delta\epsilon\lambda\tau\acute{\iota}o\nu$, V, 1896-1900, p. 223). Finally in March, 1688, Morosini reorganized San Felice's "bombisti," dividing them into six companies, each with its own captain, and providing that the Count should only assume the command when important works were in progress (*Dispacci*; second letter of March 18).

[18] The following section, from "Atene" to "mancanza de' soccorsi" (p. 15, line 8) is condensed with unimportant verbal changes and a few additions, from the much longer account of Athens—itself admittedly a much abbreviated and somewhat free translation of Spon—contained in Coronelli's *Memorie istoriografiche del Regno della Morea racquistato dall' Armi della Serenissima Republica di Venezia* (Venezia, 1688), pp. 203-210. This edition, in spite of its date, has no reference to the capture of Athens and apparently repeats an earlier text. It contains a free version of Babin's view of Athens instead of Spon's plan used by Coronelli in the earlier editions of his work (J. R. Wheeler, *Harvard Studies in Classical Philology*, VII, 1896, pp. 180-182). The first edition of the *Memorie*, published in 1686, has no mention of Athens, Piraeus, or Megara, but a French version of our text appears in the folio edition published by Coronelli in Paris in 1687. (On this edition, which Coronelli in his preface calls the sixth, see Laborde, pp. 101-102, note.)

The scanty additions made by Ivanovich are as follows:

P. 14, lines 3-5: "Di questa famossissima città - - - degna d'osservazione."

P. 14, line 11: "ma resta distrutto dalle bombe."

P. 14, lines 26-30: "Conservavano un non so che - - - Questa città è antichissima e - - -."

P. 14, line 31: The sentence "Tale fiorì - - - tempo" replaces a much longer summary of Athenian history in Coronelli.

P. 15, line 8: After "soccorsi" Coronelli continues "da quel tempo già mai dall' Impero Ottomano si disgionse," which was naturally altered by Ivanovich.

[19] In his last letter to P. Giacomo Lubrani at Naples, dated November 29, 1687, Ivanovich wrote: "Hà sigillati il Generalissimo Morosini i periodi del campaggiamento coll' acquisto della famosa Atene, che anco in ombra spira maestà, e grandezza per l' amenità delle Campagne, per la salubrità del clima, e per le dovizie delle merci, che ivi godono, una rimarcabile confluenza" (*Minerva*, II, p. 522). The *Avvisi*, also, more than once call attention to the favorable situation of Athens for the health of the army. Thus on December 3, Guasconi sent to Florence a copy of a long letter written in Athens on October 27, in which we read of "l' aria così salubre che si vedono conservati e con vigore viventi due vecchi; l' uno d' età d' anni 130, e l' altro di 118, e che non inutili alle proprie facende caminano tra monti, e resistono al grave peso delle fatiche." These two centenarians pre-

sented themselves to Morosini when he visited the city after the capitulation (Beregani, II, p. 339). Later in the same letter we read: "Le pioggie hanno dato principio, e vanno continuando, regnando sirocchi ch' annoiano, e poco proffittevoli a corpi humani particolarimente in queste parti in un clima precisamente caldo. La città però gode il vantaggio ch' essendo sotto la tramontana non tanto sogiace al tedio" (Arch. Med., 1577, No. 214 encl.; cf. also 3043, fol. 1801v, Dec. 6; Misc. Med., 667, Dec. 6; Inquisitori, Nov. 22). A month later letters from Athens of November 24 reported: "La stagione non s' era per anco data al rigore, regnando sirocchi poco buoni a sani, e pessimi a gl' ammalati, ma essendo sotto la tramontana non meno la Città d' Athene che il Porto restavano con questa conciliati li mali effetti delli medesimi" (Arch. Med., 1577, No. 228 encl.; 3043, fol. 1835r, Dec. 27).

[20] This statement is exaggerated, although the Venetian losses were certainly insignificant. The Turkish artillery, it is true, did little damage, but their musketry proved more effective. In planting the first batteries a sergeant-major and fifteen men were killed, and the attempts (omitted by Ivanovich) to construct regular approaches and drive a mine under the Acropolis caused further losses. See Laborde, p. 147, note; *Z. bild. K.*, XXII, 1887, pp. 369-370; *Ragguaglio giornaliero* in *R. ét. gr.*, VIII, 1895, p. 258; Beregani, II, pp. 336-337.

[21] These Turkish raids were sufficiently threatening to lead, as is well known, to the prompt construction of three redoubts to protect the road from Piraeus to Athens (Laborde, p. 207, note). Somewhat later, on November 14, Morosini wrote: "Per cautare nel mentre in miglior modo la comunicatione del camino lungo di qui alla Città s' è conosciuto conferente alli tre già eretti bonetti aggiongerne un altro in sito proprio, che coll' impiego della sola ciurma, e coll' assidua personal assistenza dell' Illustrissimo Signor Governatore di Galeaza Bon resta - - - perfettamente stabilito con qualch' altro lavoro, che copre, et assicura assieme questa parte di marina dagl' insulti massimi, che notte tempo fossero mai per tentarsi." Even with this protection the proximity of the enemy seems to have caused Königsmark some anxiety. The Swedish officer says (*Z. bild. K.*, XXII, 1887, p. 371) that the troops were so quartered in the city that in case of alarm the whole army could at once man the walls, and this disposition is clearly shown on Verneda's plan of Athens in the Biblioteca Marciana (*Mss. Ital.*, VII, 94, fol. 115; published B. Ebhart, *Der Burgwart*, XI, 1910,

45-49; Michaelis, *C. r. Acad. Insc.*, 1910, pp. 278-285). Furthermore Morosini abandoned his plan to impose the maintenance of the army on the citizens, partly because they could not meet so heavy a charge, but also because " trovò anco il Signor Generale dell' altre difficoltà insuperabili per lasciare disperso in tanta vicinanza de' nemici con disordine di militar disciplina in molte habitationi mischiato fra le famiglie de' Greci quel poco numero di gente" (*Dispacci*, Oct. 30, 1687).

The raids seem to have begun immediately after the futile attempt on September 28 to raise the siege, for the Swedish officer tells of one on the next day, marked by a duel between a Turk and a Sclavonian, which is also described, with some picturesque variations, in the *Avviso* of the Inquisitori for November 22. They were evidently quite frequent during the autumn and early winter, for they are mentioned several times in the letters and *Avvisi*. Thus Matteo del Teglia wrote on November 29 to Florence, " se bene i Turchi s' addomesticavano a fare nel paese qualche scorreria, non inferiscano però danno alcuno, e non tornassero a casa loro senza la peggio, da Cristiani respinti col solito loro vigoroso coraggio" (Arch. Med., 3043, fol. 1783) ; and on December 6 sent an *Avviso* which reported: " Le Truppe però erano acquartierate nella città d' Athene, e sempre all' armi per la vicinanza nella quale si trovano i Turchi con l' ardimento d' imboscate e scorrerie " (*ibid.*, fol. 1801r; Misc. Med., 667). Later in the winter the Turks were less active, for letters from Athens of February 2 announced that they " non erano però così molesti come primo in campagna per esser sempre stati buttati nelle loro scorrerie" (Inquisitori, March 13, 1687/8).

[22] The following sentence is crossed out, but is still lègible: " Misitrà, che già aveva intavolata la sua resa a Corintho, la conchiuse a descrezione con vantaggio di publico interesse e decoro." Ivanovich probably erased this passage because he had already narrated the surrender of Mistra in Book 2.

[23] The sentence enclosed in brackets is written in the margin and marked for insertion at this point. For the fate of Mistra see above, Appendix II, pp. 32-36.

[24] Megara must have been burned very soon after the capture of Athens, for in his letter of October 10 (Varola and Volpato, p. 14) Morosini, referring to the plans of Königsmark, writes: " Nell' essersi poi in questi giorni potuto incendiar totalmente la terra grossa di Megara, da loro (*i. e.* Turchi) abbandonata in vicinanza dello

stretto medesimo, pare che il Signor Generale Königsmark pensi anco all' aggressione di Tebe per distruggere quel ricovero al Seraschiere." From this letter the news passed into the *Avvisi* of the Inquisitori for November 8 (Lambros, N. E., XX, 1926, p. 213), and the little pamphlet, *Vera e distinta Relazione,* etc., p. 4. See also Arch. Med., 3043, fol. 1740v; Misc. Med., 667, Nov. 8. Its destruction was in accord with the decision of the Council of War on September 17 (see above, Chap. II, note 2).

[25] Like the preceding notices of Athens and Piraeus the following accounts of Mistra and Megara are condensed from Coronelli's *Memorie istoriografiche* (edit. 1688), pp. 90-97, 196-200. Mistra, but not Megara, first appeared in the folio edition of 1686. Coronelli's source for Mistra is certainly Guillet's *Lacédémone ancienne et nouvelle* (Paris, 1676), especially vol. II, pp. 369-372, 385-390. Indeed La Guilletière, Guillet's pseudonym, is cited for the latitude and longitude. The antiquities of Megara are those described by Pausanias, I, 40, but from whom Coronelli derived this selection I am unable to say. His account of the modern town is based on Spon (*Voyage,* Lyon, 1678, II, pp. 285-291), who, however, says nothing about the ancient monuments.

[26] This statement is wholly wrong. Mistra was peaceably surrendered by Demetrios Palaiologos to Mohammed II in 1460, and the governor of the castle was not sawn asunder (W. Miller, *The Latins in the Levant,* London, 1908, p. 447). Coronelli gives the correct date in his first folio edition, but 1465 in the later edition in octavo.

[27] In the first folio edition Coronelli gives the date as 1463, in the later editions as 1473. In fact, Mistra was attacked in 1464 (Guillet says 1463) by the Venetians commanded by Sigismondo Malatesta, who took and burned the lower town, but failed to capture the citadel before his return to Italy (Miller, *op. cit.*, pp. 467-468, note 1). I can find no mention of a Venetian general Benedetto Colleone, but the *Avviso* of the Inquisitori, dated November 1, which contains much the same résumé of the history of Mistra, says that neither Benedetto Colleone nor his successor Sigismondo could take the citadel. It thus appears that the unknown Colleone has usurped the place of Bertoldo d' Este, the predecessor of Sigismondo, who was killed in 1463 during a Venetian attack on Corinth (Miller, *op. cit.*, p. 467). There seems no evidence that he attempted Mistra.

[28] There is here a somewhat significant departure from the text of Coronelli (p. 196), where Megara is described as " Borgo si copioso

d' Abitanti, quanto numeroso di Case, che lo compongono, quali saranno quattrocento in circa fabricata per lo più di pietra cotta con coperto di fascine, assodate da cerca Terra à tal effetto usuale. I Nazionali sono Greci di gran osservanza, ne quivi s' arischiano permanervi i Turchi dopo esser stato dalli Corsari fatto schiavo il loro Vaivoda." This picture of a Greek town was hardly consistent with the explanation that Megara was burned to prevent the return of the Turks, who had abandoned it from fear of the Venetians.

[29] Here again the text of Coronelli (p. 198) gives more prominence to the Greek character of Megara. "A settentrione di questa Città sono nella pianura nove, o dieci Chiese, d' intorno alle quali v' era altri tempi una Villa detto Paleocorio hoggidì desolata, e distrutta."

[30] These dispatches were eagerly awaited at Venice, for after the arrival on August 30 of letters from Morosini announcing the capture of Corinth and his departure with the fleet for the Saronic Gulf, two months passed without other news than vague and often contradictory rumours, usually announcing the capture almost without resistance of Negroponte, brought by merchant ships from the Levant—rumours which were duly transmitted to Florence, with ever increasing scepticism, by Teglia and Guasconi. For this uncertainty Morosini was hardly to blame. During his voyage he had nothing important to report, and on September 20, just before leaving Corinth for Athens, he duly sent the Senate a detailed account of his doings, as well as of the discussions and final decisions of the Council of War. Unfortunately the feluca which bore these letters was so delayed by storms that it took forty-three days for the voyage, and did not reach Venice until Sunday, November 2, only three days before the tartana which had left Athens on October 11 (Inquisitori, Nov. 8; Teglia, Arch. Med., 3043, fols. 1727, Nov. 3; 1733, Nov. 5; Guasconi, *ibid.*, 1577, Nos. 197, 200). The departure of the latter ship was mentioned in a letter from Athens of October 27, sent to Florence by Guasconi on December 3 (Arch. Med., 1577, No. 214 encl.): "La speditione di qui della publica tartana, Santa Maria Madalena, col Capitano d' alabardieri di quest' Eccellenza fatta per avisare con dispacci a Sua Serenità l' acquisto d' Athene, etc."

NOTES TO CHAPTER III

[1] Manuscript, vol. VI, lib. i. See above, Chap. I, note 1.

[2] The *Avvisi* at Venice, Florence, and Rome show that for the most part the galleys (*armata sottile*) remained at Piraeus, although we hear that eight were detached for the chase of Turkish galeotte and to maintain a blockade of Negroponte and Monemvasia (Arch. Med., 3044, fol. 30v, Jan. 17; fol. 49, Jan. 24 = 1577, No. 243 encl.); while the ships (*armata grossa*) under Venier and Contarini cruised in the Archipelago "a riscuoter da quell' Isole le solite contribuzioni" (Arch. Med., 3043, fol. 1787v, Nov. 29, 1687; 3044, fol. 152, March 13, 1688 = 1577, No. 265 encl.), and the former also appeared off Salonica (Inquisitori, Dec. 22; Arch. Med., 3043, fol. 1835v, Dec. 27 = 1577, No. 228 encl.). For the quartering of the army in Athens see above, Chap. II, note 21.

[3] On February 12 Morosini wrote that the plague in the Morea was decreasing and that he hoped it would soon end, "presservandosi in tanto, colla protettione del Cielo, non meno l' armata di terra, che di mare immune da disastri, et in una salute, che mai nei sverni passati s' è goduta"; and on March 13 the *Avvisi* of the Inquisitori announced: "Le ultime lettere dell' armata portano che vi si goda intiera salute, anche di malatie ordinarie, e favorita dalla stagione erano già concie le galeazze, e galere sottili, eccettuatene 3." See also the *Avvisi* of the same date and tenor in Rome and Florence.

[4] The bad weather seems to have begun in February. Early in March letters from Athens, dated February 2, reached Venice bringing word "che già godevano colà la primavera, verdaggiando le campagne non havendo in tutto l' inverno veduto che un poco di neve sopra la cima de' monti, che a pena comparsa si dileguò" (Arch. Med., 1577, No. 265 at end; cf. Vitt. Eman., 756, March 13). The weather broke soon after, for the ship that brought these letters also brought from Zante an account of the storms and shipwrecks in the Gulf of Corinth. In his second letter of March 18 Morosini reported: "Scorsa buona parte del verno con placidezza de' tempi si sono poi ne' principij del scaduto mese a tal segno irrigiditi, che da venti all' estremo impetuosi insorte le più fiere tempeste han per molti giorni continuato in borasche di rotta universal fortuna, onde per appena in questo si ben chiuso porto ricovro di sicurezza si poteva pro-

228 encl.). It would seem that the Turkish commander withdrew from Thebes toward Thessaly with a view to collecting a new army to meet the next move of the Venetians. By the spring he had so far succeeded that on May 15 the *Avvisi* announced: " Il Seraschiero si trovava a Larissa con voce havesse raccolti 12,000 huomini, e questi pure gente inesperta, e publicavano di valersi introdurre in Morea " (Arch. Med., 3044, fol. 288v).

[13] According to Morosini's letter of November 14, Sain Pasha was then at Zittuni (Lamia) in Thessaly.

[14] This statement doubtless reflects a prevalent opinion in Venice, where the astonishing successes of the past few years must have created a strong belief in the incapacity of the Turks to offer any effectual resistance, but it was certainly not encouraged by Morosini. In his letter of October 10 (Varola and Volpato, pp. 15 f.) he dwells upon the need of collecting a strong force to attack Negroponte in the spring, and laments that the lack of such a force has made it impossible to take advantage of the present consternation of the enemy. On December 17 (Laborde, p. 209, note) he insists that to ensure success he will need not less than 18,000 trained soldiers. The outbreaks of plague in the Morea caused him great anxiety, as he feared they might delay the dispatch of fresh troops; the Turks were strengthening Negroponte, and if they were the first to be reinforced, they might even by their superior numbers compel him to retreat from Athens (*Dispacci*, Jan. 6). Finally in his second letter of March 18 he suggests that the veteran troops in Dalmatia be sent at once to him and the new levies on their arrival in Venice to Dalmatia, thus enabling the campaign in Greece to open earlier, and also economizing in the expense of transport (see below, Appendix IV, note 20). Incidentally this plan, which was not adopted, was admirably adapted to hamper the operations of Morosini's rival, Girolamo Cornaro, the commander in Dalmatia. In reading these letters we must bear in mind that Morosini felt it necessary to press his case strongly, yet the events of the following summer showed that he had not exaggerated his needs, nor in fact do the *Avvisi* minimize the Turkish strength in defense, although, as we have seen, they make light of the value of the field army.

[15] In his first letter of March 18 Morosini reports that among other activities the Turks " specialmente s' allestiscono 40 galeote in Costantinopoli, affine di tirannegiar non meno l' Isole d' Archipelago, che d' inferir danni et insulti gagliardi alle rive tutte di Morea." The

galeotta was a relatively small galley, having about 30 or 40 oars. The *leventi* were the fighting crew of the galley. They usually numbered about 80. See N. Barozzi e G. Berchet, *Le Relazioni degli Stati Europei lette al Senato degli Ambasciatiori Veneziani nel secolo decimosettimo* (Venezia, 1856-74), Serie V, Turchia, vol. I, 2, p. 336, G. Donato, 1684: " chi milita sul mare viene nominato col titolo di Levente "; p. 20, G. Capello, 1634: " Il numero ordinario de' soldati sopra ogni una galera è di 80."

[16] These Bulgarians had apparently been aroused by the arrival of Venier's squadron off Salonica (Chap. III, note 2), for the *Avvisi* of late December report: " S' erano offerti alcuni habitanti di Bulgheria, che stanno a Salonichi nel luogo detto Partanona (v. 1. Passavona, Patanora; probably the modern Platamona), di passare a servire nell' armata in qualità di Venturieri con 300 cavalli, ed altretanti fanti, e gli erano state accordate capitolationi honorevoli, e riconosciuti gl' Inviati con medaglie d' oro " (Arch. Med., 1577, No. 228 encl., Dec. 27; cf. *ibid.*, 3043, fol. 1835v; Misc. Med., 667, Dec. 27; Inquisitori, Dec. 22, 26). In the spring new approaches were made, and on March 13 the Inquisitori announced: " Le ultime lettere dell' armata portano - - - che verso le parti di Salonicchio erano insorte nuove sollevationi, e precisamente Frango homo di gran stima - - - si era fatto vedere alla nostra armata, ove era stato ben accolto, e regalato di medaglie d' oro, havendo promesso di far gran cosa." Locatelli (II, p. 35) says that the Bulgarian captain, Francesco Maidan, from Scopelos came to Athens in December, asking for arms and ammunition for a large force, which he claimed to have collected, and also for permission to keep all the booty. He was assured of help, if he kept his promises, but nothing more is heard of him. The arrival of a Pasha to repress the revolt and round up the recalcitrant contingent from Negroponte was reported in an *Avviso* of April 10 (Arch. Med., 3044, fol. 970v), but three months later Venice heard that the Christians were in revolt from Salonica to Valona (Inquisitori, July 3), that the Bulgarians were still calling upon the fleet to come to their aid (Arch. Med., 3044, fol. 468, July 31), and finally the welcome, but unfortunately false, news that Morosini had been joined at Negroponte by 5000 Albanian infantry and 3000 cavalry (Teglia, Arch. Med., 3044, fol. 486, Aug. 11). It seems very doubtful whether this Bulgarian revolt ever came to a head. Certainly it was never serious enough to be of any real assistance to the Venetians.

[17] The surrender of Nauplia on August 28, 1686, and the appear-

ance somewhat later of Morosini's galleys at Porto Raphti (Foscarini, p. 278; Locatelli, I, p. 280; cf. Mateses in Kampouroglos, Μνημεῖα τῆς ἱστορίας τῶν Ἀθηναίων, I, p. 91), naturally alarmed the Turks of Negroponte, and they began at once to strengthen their defences by fortifying the hill on the mainland which commanded the entrance to the bridge over the Euripus (Arch. Med., 1577, No. 125, June 18, 1687: " Altra [lettera] d' Atene dice che avanti il ponte per cui si passa nell' Isola di Negroponte vi erigessero li Turchi un gran forte per difesa "). The fall of Athens, which obviously brought the danger of an attack very near, only stimulated their efforts. On December 26 the Inquisitori heard from Athens: " Che in Negroponte si continuavano i lavori per la diffesa di quell' importante piazza " (also under Dec. 27 in Arch. Med., 3043, fol. 1835v; 1577, No. 228 encl.; Misc. Med., 667), and on May 15, 1688, they were able to sum up the work which had been accomplished, as follows: " Perchè la vicinanza dell' armata a Negroponte faceva temer a' Turchi, che dovesse cader sopra quel regno il primo dissegno, facevano ogni sforzo per mettersi in difesa; onde vi havevano introdotta gente raccolta in quelle parti come havevano potuto, aggiungendo lavori alla nova Fortezza di Carabagdà (*i. e.* Kara Babà) ellevata (minata, Vitt. Eman.) parte della città, e palificata all' intorno, et alzata qualche batteria al porto, operationi tutte fatte con la direttione d' un tal rinegato Galoppo, che servendo d' Aiutante nella nostra armata era fugito alla parte de' Turchi, spacciandosi per ingegniere, et accolto da medesimi si valsero nella mancanza che hanno d' huomini d' esperienza " (also Arch. Med., 3044, fol. 288r; 1577, No. 305 encl.; Vitt. Eman., 756. The clause " si valsero - - - esperienza " is here added from Arch. Med., 3044).

Girolamo Galoppo of Guastalla, between Mantua and Parma, was a dragoon in Corbon's regiment and a gambler, who had fled to Negroponte during the siege of Nauplia, alleging in excuse for his desertion that he could no longer endure the ill-treatment of Daniel Dolfin, whose Adjutant he had been (Foscarini, p. 388; Locatelli, I, p. 234). Locatelli adds that strenuous though futile efforts were made to capture him, as he had some knowledge of the principles of fortification. If he really inspired the Turks to build Kara Babà, he was in large measure responsible for their successful defense in 1688, since this fort, which secured the continuous passage into the city of the necessary supplies and reinforcements, proved an insurmountable obstacle to the beseigers. This was clearly recognized later, for we learn from Matteo del Teglia that when the news of the failure reached Venice and public opinion turned against Morosini, his errors were held to have caused the disaster, and in particular: " L' unica cagione di molti danni si riconosce ancora dalla ruvida maniera di Sua Serenità con ogni ordine di persone, di come più volte lo si sono espressi ne' publici circoli ufficiali di condizione e Venturieri; e 'l mal esito di questa spirata campagna si riconosce meramente allo strapazzo d' un ufficiale francese (Galoppo was not French but Italian) l' anno passato all' attacco di Napoli di Romania, ponendolo in dispositione di disertare alla parte nemica dove servendo d' ingeniere, oltre molte difese aggiunte alle città di Negroponte, vi costruiva quel forte esteriore, che ha impedito a' Christiani l' acquisto della piazza; e questa è istoria verissima, di cui ne ho più volte scrisso, e ne haverà Vostra Illustrissima molti riscontri " (Arch. Med., 3044, fols. 729 f., Dec. 1, 1688). In spite of Teglia's affirmation, we need not believe that Morosini rather than Dolfin was responsible for Galoppo's desertion; but that the charge was made at all shows what importance was attached to his work.

[18] For the transport of the army to the island of Poros see Appendix IV, pp. 43-46.

[19] The passage in brackets is written in the margin but marked for insertion at this point. Although the decision to appoint the Catasticatori was adopted by the Senate on September 4, 1687 (Arch. Med., 3043, fol. 1614), and was enthusiastically welcomed by Morosini in his letter of October 11 (Lambros, N.E., XVIII, 1924, p. 263), apparently nothing further was done until the late winter, when Garzoni (pp. 260 f.) records the election of the three Catasticatori and defines their duties as follows: " Per mettere à regola l' economia, e dalla maniera tirannica ridurre que' popoli alla retta della Repubblica, vennero spediti tre Senatori, Girolamo Renier, Domenico Gritti, e Marino Michele col titolo volgare di Sindici, e Catasticatori. Loro assunto dovea essere di riparare il Regno in territorj con i suoi confini, formar disegni, e catalogi de' beni, nelle Città rilevare gli edificj, che fossero proprj à convertirsi in Chiese Latine, in domicilj de' Religiosi, in abitazioni di pubblici Rappresentanti, e Ministri, in quartieri de' soldati, e in magazzini da munizioni: imporre decime, ò altro aggravio a' terreni de' Greci, confiscare que' de' Turchi, e ricuperargli da gli usurpatori: instituire Camere per l' esazione de' dritti: imporre Dazj, e procacciare vantaggi al commercio." In view of this formidable programme, it is hardly surprising that the

new officials showed no haste to enter upon their duties, and in fact did not reach the Morea until August, 1688 (Lambros, N. E., XX, 1926, p. 57; letter from Patras, August 18). Lambros has published a summary of many of their letters to the Senate, *ibid.*, pp. 56 ff., 193 ff., and the final report of Marino Michiel, dated Coron, November 29, 1691, in his Ἱστορικὰ Μελετήματα, pp. 199-220.

[20] The prominence given to the contingent sent by the Duke of Parma, who incidentally was not the only Italian prince to aid the Venetians, seems to be due rather to the attachment of Ivanovich to the ducal house than to the importance of the contribution itself. It accords well with his dedication of the *Poesie* to Ranuccio II and of the first volume of the *Minerva al tavolino* to his three sons. It may be doubted whether Ranuccio was animated purely by his affection for Venice. He was engaged in a dispute with Cosimo III as to the boundary between Parma and Tuscany in the neighborhood of Pontremoli, and Venice had been asked to arbitrate. Under these conditions he might well feel that it was prudent to match the Florentine contingent with one from Parma.

[21] Giorgio Emo, appointed Commissario Pagatore in 1683 (Foscarini, p. 177), had been with Morosini since the beginning of the war in 1684, and the latter devotes a considerable part of his letter of November 15, 1687, to a eulogy of his conduct during forty-two months of service in his difficult and responsible position. His departure ought chronologically to have been mentioned much earlier, for his recall was reported to the Council of War by Morosini on September 30, and he left Athens to enter upon his new duties about November 13 (Locatelli, II, p. 14), arriving in Venice about a month later (Vitt. Eman., 755, Dec. 20). The appointment of Nani as his successor is reported by Morosini in his letter of November 15. Locatelli's statement that the appointment was given to Pietro Querini is clearly incorrect.

[22] On Wednesday, March 24, 1688, Guasconi wrote to the Abate Bassetti at Florence: " Rese poi hier sera verso le quattro della notte l' anima santa a Dio il Doge Serenissimo, compianto universalmente da tutti per la sua degnissima qualità, et è notabile che mentre Sabato haveva preso migliormente e che un suo cameriere confidente si rallegrava seco di ciò e lo animava, gli rispose Sua Serenità ' Antonio, non dureremo che Domenica, Lunedì, e Martedì.' Non si pubblicherà la sua morte che Sabato mattina per dar tempo a suoi di sgomberare il Palazzo. Già i nepoti e parenti del Signor Capitano Generale Moro-

sini sono in broglio, e tutti gl' altri concorrenti sono questa mattina stati a offerirli i lor voti, onde si fa conto che Domenica a otto sarà già eletto, e si saprà il ceremoniale che doverà praticarsi, e si sente che non sarà di quel dispendio pubblico che si era decantato " (Arch. Med., 1577, No. 272).

[23] On Saturday, March 27, Guasconi again wrote to Florence: " Questa mattina si è publicata la morte del Serenissimo Doge, chi è esposto in publico. Dimani sarà Consiglio per eleggere cinque Correttori e due Inquisitori; Martedì si farà la ceremonia del interramento, e poi susseguiranno i Consigli per l' eletione del nuovo Doge, che sarà fatto per domani a otto, e sarà il Signor Capitano Generale Morosini applaudito da tutti degniamente." A week later on April 3, he sent a long account of the election, which had been completed more quickly than he had expected (Arch. Med., 1577, Nos. 274, 277).

For the ceremonies which followed the death of a Doge and for the complicated system of balloting by which his successor was chosen, see, for example, F. Mutinelli, *Lessico Veneto* (Venezia, 1852), *s. v.* Doge; H. F. Brown, *Venice: An historical Sketch* (London, 1895), pp. 150-151. Judging from Teglia's account of the election of Morosini (see above, pp. 47-48), it would seem that intrigue and bargaining were not seriously hindered by the system.

[24] On April 7 Matteo del Teglia wrote to Florence: " Essendosi per tre giorni festeggiata in Casa Morosini, e di varii suoi congiunti l' elettione del nuovo Serenissimo Doge, lo spettacolo è non men bello che curioso nel misto di baccanali di maschere, di giuoco e di ballo, con le processioni del popolo divoto ai perdoni diversi della città, la quale produce sola queste stravaganze " (Arch. Med., 3044, fol. 197). The election took place in Lent, hence the contrast between the crowds of revellers and of penitents, which so impressed Teglia.

[25] On the election of Morosini see Appendix IV, pp. 47 ff., and note 22 above.

parole " and " pesante maneggio " appear in the passage quoted above (p. 33) from the minutes of the Council of War, which in spite of its gracious words really only promises the inhabitants their lives, since the exercise of the " generosa clemenza " lies wholly in the discretion of the Council. Later, after describing the abandonment of the women and old men at the Piraeus, Muazzo continues: "Acciò perissero dentro l' infezioni del loco, et si registrasse colà un fatto sì empio, forse perchè le conclusioni della guerra più atroce lo retribuissero nell' occasioni venturi " (fol. 62r = Paris, fol. 28v), and finally pronounces this verdict on the fate of Mistra and Athens: " I Mistriotti affidorono nella Christiana Carità, obligata in scrittura donarli vita e libertà, li Atteniesi dalla stessa assicurati accolsero il Morosini, acciò la patria e la religione li difendesse. Ma con Grandi la fede del patuito non basta " (fol. 63v = Paris, fol. 29v). Muazzo was undoubtedly no friend of Morosini and little disposed to admit extenuating circumstances, but even so it must be admitted that in this case his severe judgment was not without justification.

NOTES TO APPENDIX III

[1] Laborde, p. 170, note.

[2] *Ibid.*, pp. 191-197, note.

[3] *Ibid.*, pp. 198-200, note.

[4] *Ibid.*, pp. 202-204, note. The date, February 2, given by Laborde must be that of the receipt in Venice. The copy in the Civico Museo, *Mss. Correr*, 299, is dated January 6, and the news it contained was sent to Florence by Guasconi on February 4 and by Teglia on February 7, but without mention of the plague by either.

[5] Arch. Med., 3044, fol. 79r, February 7, 1687/8.

[6] *Ibid.*, 1577, no. 248: " Si sono riceute lettere del Signor Capitano Generale delli 6 Gennaio e come che pare che tutta la sua mira per la prossima campagnia tende sopra Negroponte, motiva anche che non stimando di poter haver gente bastante per quell' impresa, e per coprire la città d' Atene, che per esser aperta vuol un corpo di gente valido per guardarla, andava pensando se per non esponer quei popoli a una sorpresa de' Turchi in sua absenza, dovesse condurli in sicuro in qualche altro luogo; dall' altro canto il lasciare in abbandono un così bello e ricco paese haverebbe molto rincresciuto, e gli è però credibile nel stato che sono le cose de' Turchi, che se li nostri si porteranno ad attacare Negroponte, anch' essi saranno obligati di accorrere con tutte le sue forze alla difesa di quel regno, senza poter pensare a disturbare Atene."

[7] Arch. Med., 1577, No. 249.

[8] Morosini, *Dispacci* = Lambros, N. E., XVIII, 1924, pp. 267 f.

[9] Laborde, p. 172, note.

[10] Inquisitori, March 13; cf. Arch. Med., 1577, No. 265 encl.; 3044, fol. 152r; Vitt. Eman., 756.

[11] Arch. Med., 1577, No. 264, March 10; 276, March 31 encl.; 280, April 7 encl.

[12] Bulifon, *Lettere memorabili*, in Laborde, p. 190, note; Mateses, in Kampouroglos, Ἱστορία, I, p. 144 = Μνημεῖα, I, p. 91.

[13] Mateses in Kampouroglos, *loc. cit.*

[14] Inquisitori, April 10; Arch. Med., 1577, No. 283 encl.; 3044, fol. 970.

[15] Vitt. Eman., 756, February 21.

[16] Locatelli, II, p. 34.

[17] *Dispacci*; cf. Laborde, p. 204, note.

[18] Locatelli, II, p. 36.

[19] Laborde, pp. 210-216, note.

[20] Locatelli, II, p. 49.

[21] This letter seems to have been deemed sufficient warrant for official assurances to Guasconi of the perfect health of the army and navy, and of the disappearance of the plague in the Morea, so that the Grand Duke need feel no anxiety about sending the Florentine contingent to Morosini (Arch. Med., 1577, No. 295, April 26, 1688).

[22] The " Alfiere " may well be the Hessian Ensign, Hombergk: see Laborde, p. 351, note 2, where the date of his death is given as April first.

[23] Bulifon, *Lettere memorabili*, in Laborde, p. 190, note.

[24] Morosini, *Dispacci*, April 15, from Porto Poro: " Essequitosi l' imbarco la mattina di 8 corrente s' habbi nella sera stessa potuto prosperamente qui approdare." Königsmark left on April 6 (Anna Akerhjelm in Laborde, p. 316). Bulifon's officer on April 7 (Laborde, p. 190, note).

[25] Morosini, *Dispacci*, April 15, 1688.

[26] To the Council of War on April 18 Morosini told a somewhat different story, for he then reported that cases had appeared on thirteen of the transports and also on one galeazza and ten galleys. It would appear that new cases had been discovered in the interval of three days between the letter to the Senate and the meeting of the Council.

[27] It must be kept in mind that Morosini resented his inability to control the discipline of the German troops, who could only be punished by their own officers. His letters contain many complaints on this point. (See below, Appendix IV, note 32.)

[28] Arch. Med., 1577, No. 301; 3044, fol. 267.

[29] *Ibid.*, 1577, No. 304.

[30] *Ibid.*, 3044, fol. 267v.

[31] *Ibid.*, 1656, May 8, 1688.

[32] *Ibid.*, 3044, fol. 275r.

[33] *Ibid.*, 3044, fol. 390v.

[34] *Ibid.*, 3044, fol. 387v. Guasconi, 1577, No. 323, was better informed, for he says that there had been 33 deaths on the fleet and 540 on land.

[35] *Ibid.*, 3044, fol. 395v.

[36] *Ibid.*, 1577, No. 346, August 14. Guasconi reports that he has seen a letter of the Doge's Secretary from Porto Poro, dated July 6, in which he says: " Dimani si farà vela per Negroponte, impresa dura e difficile, e che ha bisogno di una grand' assistenza del Cielo." This departure was confirmed by a letter from Zante on July 18.

NOTES TO APPENDIX IV

[1] Arch. Med., 3044, fols. 189-190.

[2] In his letter of March 31 (*ibid.*, fols. 182-183), Teglia wrote that the " Casa " had generously promised that Morosini, if he were elected, would draw only his pay as Captain General, so long as he remained at the head of the army in the Levant, surrendering to the State his salary as Doge, while continuing to meet, even in his absence, the expenses at the Palace usually borne by the Doge, amounting to upwards of 20,000 ducats a year. Indeed Teglia seems to have felt some doubt whether without these liberal offers Morosini's public services alone would have secured his election.

[3] The names of the forty-one electors are given on folio 191.

[4] In his letter of April 7 (*ibid.*, fol. 197v) Teglia again enlarges on the limitations to the power of the Doge. The formal announcement to Morosini of his election has been delayed " per l' elettione che deve farsi nel Maggiore Consiglio di due Consiglieri che si mandano con un' Segretario per assistere alla Serenità sua nella direttione delle cose, non dovendo sua Serenità partire d' armata senza la permissione dello stesso Maggiore Consiglio, e le resolutioni degli affari doveranno passare con la ballottatione di sua Serenità, i dui Consiglieri, e del Proveditore d' Armata doppo la consulta degli altri Capi ch' hanno l' introduzione nel Consulta di Guerra senza voto deliberativo, di modo che la Serenità sua avanza tanto di posto, quanto scapita d' autorità in questa sua esaltatione, benchè ciò segua per ordine di formalità, e non si perda punto della stima che si ha della Serenità sua." The two Councillors were Girolamo Grimani and Lorenzo Donato, and it was also provided that in case of a tie the Doge had a deciding vote (Garzoni, p. 263).

After Morosini's death a law was passed to prevent the Doge from holding the office of Captain General (*ibid.*, pp. 512-513).

[5] In his letter of March 24 (Arch. Med., 3044, fol. 167) announcing the death of the Doge, Teglia expressed his belief that Morosini would be elected without opposition, for Cornaro's party, which was diametrically opposed to Morosini and numerous (*ibid.*, fol. 182v), would favor his election, in the hope that he would return to Venice and that Cornaro would then be chosen Captain General—a hope which was fulfilled in 1689.

[6] Arch. Med., 3042, fol. 734v, July 22, 1684, where Teglia distinctly attributes to this motive Cornaro's premature attack on Santa Maura, which he himself feared would lead the Turks so to strengthen their defences as to make its capture impossible.

[7] Foscarini, p. 182, who, however, says nothing about Cornaro's jealousy, but merely that he was deceived by false reports.

[8] Beregani, I, p. 290, says that late in 1685 Giacomo Cornaro was appointed Proveditore Generale dell' Isole in succession to Girolamo.

[9] Foscarini, p. 259.

[10] Foscarini, p. 335, indicates that Morosini's friends thought the importance of this event was exaggerated: " Hebbe però in Venetia applauso questa difesa per le relationi vantaggiose, che furono publicate, e perchè i partiali della gloria del Cornaro, che procuravano interessare il Senato ad assistergli con gente, e munitioni amplificavano ogni successo." Foscarini was an ardent admirer of Morosini and intended to dedicate his work to the Doge. His history was unfinished at his death, but his brother completed and published it with the dedication, although Morosini himself had already died.

[11] This refusal, with the consequent diversion of other reinforcements from the Levant, was certainly displeasing to Morosini, for it meant a reduction of over 4000 men in his small army. According to Foscarini (pp. 337-338) and Garzoni (pp. 223-224) the united Maltese, Papal, and Florentine contingents amounted to 1800 men, while 2500 infantry, which had been intended for the Levant, were also sent from Venice to Dalmatia. Apparently Morosini felt that he could not protest openly, for the withdrawal of the auxiliaries was due to the orders of their own governments, not of Venice. He showed plainly his dissatisfaction, however, by rarely neglecting a suitable occasion for pointing out in the Council of War or in his letters to the Senate that had he had more troops he could have taken advantage of the unusually favorable conditions and ended the campaign by the capture of Negroponte as well as of Athens, while the loss of this opportunity would make it necessary to collect a much larger force, if the place was to be taken in the next campaign. See Laborde, notes on pp. 126, 127, 164, 167, 170; Varola and Volpato, pp. 12, 16 f.; Morosini, *Dispacci,* December 17, February 12; also the letter of Guasconi, quoted below, note 29.

[12] As the Maltese refused to take orders from a Proveditore Generale, Cornaro was given the authority in Dalmatia of a Capitano Generale for this campaign (Foscarini, p. 338).

[13] On August 2 Teglia wrote that one of the Savii, Giovanni Grimani, had asked him to transmit to the Grand Duke, in the name of the whole board, the following request: " Che si voglia degnare di concedere per l' impresa stabilita di Castel Novo il suo bravo bombista Amburghese, se non erro, o Brandenburghese, che sia, con qual numero d' aiutanti che il medesimo stimerà sufficiente al proprio servizio, poichè sendo il Conte di San Felice in Levante con tutti quelli subalterni, di che potessero valersi, ne sono affatto sprovisti per il presente bisogno, perchè supplicano questi Signori Sua Altissima Serenissima della gratia che sperano benignamente ottenere." Teglia adds that acquiescence will not only win the public favor, but also the gratitude of the great families of Grimani and Cornaro, which are closely connected, General Cornaro being the uncle of the Savio Grimani. On August 16 Teglia reported the joy and gratitude of the Savii on learning that their request had been granted (Arch. Med., 3043, fols. 1544, 1565).

[14] *Ibid.*, fols. 1627-1629. It is interesting to compare the popular opinion at this time as to the value of Morosini's victories with the revulsion of feeling, as reported by Teglia, after the failure at Negroponte, when it was said that this defeat would make it very difficult and expensive to maintain the conquests in Greece, and that it was now clear that Castel Nuovo was really the most important acquisition, since Dalmatia could be more easily and cheaply defended (*ibid.*, 3044, fol. 729v, December 1, 1688).

[15] *Ibid.*, 3043, fols. 1635-1636, September 20, 1687. The first reports were that the place itself had been stormed, but it was later learned that only some of the important outer forts had been taken.

[16] Foscarini, p. 344. Morosini on receiving the news of the capture ordered a special service of thanksgiving and a *feu de joie* (*Dispacci*, November 15, 1687).

[17] Inquisitori, October 31, 1687.

[18] Arch. Med., 3043, fols. 1715-1716, October 29, 1687.

[19] This bitter comment on Morosini's motives in asking to be relieved of his command was repeated by Teglia on November 3, after the receipt of the letter of September 20 (see below): " La forza delle lettere di Sua Eccellenza s' estende in procurare la permissione di ripatriare, protestando non potere più sostenere il peso delle fatiche; ma forse quando saprà l' esaltazione del rivale, chi le doverà in tal caso succedere, si lascerà persuadere a restar nella carica, che con artificio mostra volere lasciare per esservi confermato " (*ibid.*,

3043, fol. 1727v). Such comments were doubtless current at this time among Morosini's enemies, for during the past summer he had three times renewed this request, when there was obviously no probability of its being granted. At least this was the opinion of Guasconi, who wrote on August 10, after the victory of Patras, "Il Capitano Generale dimanda di nuove la sua licenza, ma Vostra Signoria Illustrissima pensi se si vogli dargliela"; and on August 13, that the Grand Council had voted, " sopra la licenza che con premura ricerca si procurerà farli conoscere che il Publico Bene non può mai permetterlo." Again on August 30, after summarizing Morosini's letters announcing his intention to sail around the Morea, he adds: " Per ultima [lettera] rinnuova le sue premurosissime instanze per la licenza dicendo esser incapace di più servire, massime per il solito suo male di vertigini che più che mai la travaglia. Ma il vedersi che egli opera con una previdenza e prudenza mostruosa, persuade anzi che egli stia più d' ogn' altro bene della testa, e non si puole ne si vuole per il ben della Patria esaudirlo " (ibid., 1577, Nos. 150, 153, 162). The third request was in Morosini's second letter of September 20 (Laborde, pp. 130-131, note) in which he complained that constant worry over the lack of money and supplies had so impaired his health that he must inevitably turn over the command to the Proveditor Garzoni, as the burden of responsibility was more than he could bear. The arrival of this letter, which called forth the remark of Teglia quoted above, was also reported by Guasconi with another explanation, which may perhaps have found some favor among the friends of Morosini: " Il motivo principale della spedizione [della feluca] apparisce sia per domandare, come fa con vivissime instanze, la sua licenza e il pretesto è di gravi sue indisposizioni, ma qualcheduno non lascia di dire, che molto gli sia rincresciuto l' haver inteso, che qui si havesse stabilito di mandar in Dalmatia la gente già destinata per Levante; si crede però che il Senato in nessun modo sia per concedergliela " (Arch. Med., 1577, No. 197, November 3, 1687).

Teglia's expectations were not fulfilled. In his second letter of April 15, 1688, Morosini asks the Senate to consider the choice of a successor, so that he may retire after the coming campaign.

[20] The weakening of the army in Dalmatia is confirmed by the same *Avviso* of the Inquisitori which announced the honors voted to Cornaro (note 17 above) : " Non si sono per anco imbarcati per Levante il 300 fanti mandati dal Principe di Baraith, nè ciò si farà, se prima

non giongono li 500 rimanenti della sua levata; per l' imbarco de' quali si sono fermate a buon conto 3 Tartane, e passando per Dalmatia, doveranno colà levare quelli di tal natione, che hanno travagliato all' espugnatione di quella piazza, a fine tutti uniti condurli al sbarco dove verrà dal Signore Capitan Generale comandato." In a letter of February 7, 1688, Guasconi reports a vote in the Senate to send to Athens 2000 veterans from Dalmatia and replace them by new levies (Arch. Med., 1577, No. 249), a plan also suggested by Morosini in his second letter of March 18 (see above, Chap. III, note 14).

[21] *Ibid.*, 3043, fols. 1737-1738.

[22] Guasconi devoted much space in his letters of January 14 and 16 (*ibid.*, 1577, Nos. 236, 238) to the plans for the next campaign and the disputes of the parties, evidently arousing thereby anxiety in Florence as to the future, for on January 20 Abate Bassetti replied: " Nè so se possa tornar' bene il lasciar' che si dividono in partite gli affezionati al Capitano Generale ed al Signore Generale Cornaro, perchè in tal caso le passioni della parzialità non lasciano vedere con occhio chiaro il vero interesse di Stato " (*ibid.*, No. 237).

[23] *Ibid.*, 1577, No. 233.

[24] *Ibid.*, 1577, No. 249, February 7, 1687/8. It should be added that as late as March 20, when the decision had already been taken, in accordance with the wishes of Morosini, to concentrate every effort in an attack on Negroponte, Teglia wrote that letters from Constantinople reported that the Grand Vizier intended to make the next campaign chiefly against the Venetians and to attempt the reconquest of the Morea (*ibid.*, 3044, fol. 159).

[25] *Ibid.*, 1577, No. 252.

[26] *Ibid.*, 3044, fol. 159, March 20, 1688. The reports of the prevalence of the plague in the Morea and in the army at Athens, as well as the news that the Turks were gathering a strong force to defend Negroponte, led the amateur strategists of Venice, but apparently not the Senate, to advance the theory that it would be best merely to feign an attack on Negroponte, and to use the fleet for a descent on Scio—a plan carried out in 1694 with no further result than a massacre of the Greeks when the Turks returned after the withdrawal from the island of the Venetians—or better yet for the surprise of Tenedos as probably the easier and more important conquest, since the threat to Constantinople would force the Turks to withdraw troops from Scio and even Negroponte, and thus leave

the sea open for any movement of the fleet which promised to produce good results. Teglia's comment is: " Così la discorrono, forse a capricio, i speculatori di qualche buona cognizione, di modo che non saria tanto difficile che s' indovinasse qualchuno" (*ibid.*, fol. 275, May 12, 1688).

[27] Garzoni, pp. 288 ff.; Foscarini, p. 403, with the comment, " scarsa frutta di gran dispendio." A report of this siege in diary form is in Arch. Med., 3044, fols. 589-598.

[28] See Teglia's remarks quoted above, Chap. III, note 17. Later in the same letter he says, " tale è la natura di questo Principe, che s' è sempre fatto più temere che amare."

[29] A somewhat striking example of such an outburst is found at the end of his letter from Athens written on October 11. After renewing the expressions of fervent gratitude which he had already addressed on September 20 to the Doge and Senate for their kindness and generosity in bestowing such honors on him, his nephew, and his whole family after the victory at Patras, he continues: " È però fatalità mostruosa, che tali e tanti preciosissimi indulti non bastano ancora a placar l' infierito destino, che sempre con insidiosi oltraggi cerca d' abbatermi, et a ragione ramaricarmene devo, se nell' auge delle felicità veggo senza salvezza la mia sorte, servendomi d' esemplare crucioso l' attentato promosso alla persona del Signor Cavaliere, primo de' nipoti, che mentre qui meco sta esposto a continui travagli, patimenti, et azzardi, fu quasi dalla carica di Capitano in Golfo degradato; onde ben comprendo, che la mia longa permanenza in questo elevato riguardevole impiego coll' obligo d' essercitar quella giustitia, che a tutti non piace, sia un mantice di damnosi influssi alla posterità, che mai dovrebbe per causa della pontualità e rettitudine mia nel sostener le ragioni del publico servizio soggiaceve a malvaggi disastri, dal che rissentono pure vehemente impulso le mie vivissime necessità d' esser una volta da si spinoso e grand' incargo sollevato; e se hora col secondo gionger dalla stagione infesta va notabilmente peggiorando la mia depressa e sconvolta salute per l' aumento inveterato del mal de' vertigini, ben dovrò confidere che in fine l' humanità pietosa dell' Eccellenze Vostre si mova a redimer il deplorabile mio stato, che senza questo provido, e sollecito soccorso non può, che all' estremo eccidio condurmi."

How this complaint struck a fairly impartial critic may be seen from the following comments of Guasconi (Arch. Med., 1577, No. 201, November 8, 1687): " Finalmente anco gl' huomini grandi hanno le loro passioni, e si lasciano delle medesime dominare. Il Signore Capitano Generale nell' istesso tempo che ringratia il Senato delli onori compartiti con tanta generosità a lui e alli suoi nepoti, passa a lagniarsi che il maggiore di essi fusse, mentre era già eletto Capitano in Golfo, nominato in Senato per la carica di Capitano di Galeazza, carica inferiore, allargandosi a dire che si conosceva non esser spenta l' invidia e mala volontà de' suoi emoli, mentre vedeva che havevano dato buon numero di voti in tal occasione a detto suo nepote, e che però si vedeva in obligo di tanto più desiderare la sua licenza per la quale replicava le instanze, dicendo anco che l' haver divertita altrove la gente che era destinata per lui haveva cagionato che non fusse potuta fare l' impresa di Negroponte; e parsa a tutti imprudentissima la doglianza, mentre gl' onori ottenuti ben si sono munificenza del Senato, ma non già si può dolere del publico se in una Republica ove ogn' uno ha la voce e il voto libero, sia stato nominato un suo nepote a una carica senza che sia però stato dalle pluralità eletto, e il pretendere che tutti lo stimano e lo venerino è vanità."

Pietro Morosini had been rewarded with the title of Consigliere by the Great Council (Misc. Med., 667, August 13, 1687); but in spite of his having held the rank of Capitano in Golfo, he had been nominated, but not elected, for the lower position of Capitano di Galeazza. His uncle evidently considered this nomination an intentional affront, whereby his enemies sought to strike him through his nephew—a view apparently held also by his friends, since the proposal was defeated.

[30] Varola and Volpato, p. 12. He only regrets that thus has vanished the opportunity for " un incontro che nell' attuale costernatione de' nemici più favorevole già mai potrebbe sperarsi."

[31] See, for example, the contract with the Duke of Brunswick-Lüneburg, Laborde, p. 75, note, § 9.

[32] On these controversies see Laborde, pp. 205-207, 208-209, notes. How Morosini's conduct was viewed by his critics is shown by Teglia's comments on a dispute which had arisen in 1686. Morosini had hanged a deserter from a Brunswick regiment, and the officers had vigorously protested against this violation of their contract: " Onde si sta dibattendo la materia nella quale si trova motivo di discorso sopra la natura troppo violente del Signor Capitan Generale, che ha poco riguardo a disgustare i Capi forestieri, con poco avvantagio della Republica, che ne ha bisogno, senza di che poche imprese farebbe; ma tanto partito ha Sua Eccellenza in Senato, e tanta stima

in publico, che tutto si risolve a sua favore" (Arch. Med., 3043, fol. 897v, August 17, 1686).

There would seem to have been further trouble during 1687, for in February, 1688, when the Senate was considering the appointment of a second in command to Königsmark, Teglia wrote: " Il Signor Principe di Bransvich ne raccomanda qualche uno ma esso recusa tornarvi, poco bene parlando con gli amici della cortesia del Signore Capitano Generale; può esser però che le conditioni della Republica e la dispositione del Serenissimo suo padre (non però molto gustato) lo disponga e lo persuada" (Arch. Med., 3044, fol. 79v, February 7, 1687/8). In spite of his dissatisfaction Brunswick did return to the army before it left Poros for Negroponte (*ibid.*, 3044, fols. 334, June 2; 499, August 14, 1688).

[33] Teglia, *ibid.*, 3044, fol. 722, November 27, 1688; Foscarini, p. 402.

[34] Garzoni, p. 511.

[35] *Clio Presaga nelle Nozze felicissime Degl' Illustrissimi Signori Marino, e Paolina Grimani. Oda Epitalamica di Christoforo Ivanovich.* Venetia, 1666. In the short preface, addressed to Marino, he says " la sua dignissima Persona, e Casa con tratti generosi hà sempre meco reso insuperabile la propria benignità."

[36] Sinj: *Minerva*, II, pp. 60-61, letter 41, May 5, 1687. In this letter he says, " Ella col togliere la mia Patria nel passato Campeggiamento à i rischi dell' Assedio, che le piantava Soliman Agà, Bassà di Scutari in Albania, impresse nella mia anima un carattere di perpetuo rimarco." Castel Nuovo: *ibid.*, p. 64, letter 43, October 9, 1687. The election as Procurator: *ibid.*, p. 68, letter 45, October 28, 1687.

[37] For these poems see Medin, *op. cit.*, pp. 552, 553. Medin strangely omits all reference to the poems in *Minerva*, I and II.

[38] *Minerva*, II, pp. 16-45, letters 10-24. Other poems by him, written in 1685 and 1687 (the latter on the victory at Patras) were published in *Tributo di Pindo, nell' incoronazione del Serenissimo Prencipe di Venezia, Francesco Morosini, raccolta da G.-A. Ninfa.* Venezia, 1690. See Medin, *op. cit.*, pp. 557, 560.

[39] *Minerva*, II, pp. 306-308, letter 145, November 6, 1687. The statue was, of course, voted for the victory at Patras, not the capture of Athens. Ivanovich also sent Pesaro three Latin inscriptions, long, medium, and short, which he had composed for the statue. The shortest reads FRANCISCO MAUROCENO | IMPERIO CLARO | TRIUMPHIS CLARIORI | VIVENTI S. CONSULTUM.

[40] See above, p. 20.

[41] See above, p. 26.

INDEX

INDEX

ACROPOLIS. Siege, 10-12, 69-73. Description, 13.
ATHENS. Occupied by Venetians, 10, 66, 68. Description, 13, 74. Climate, 13, 14, 74. Monuments, 14. History, 14, 15. Decision to abandon, 20, 37-38, 91. Removal of Greeks, 38, 39. Departure of Venetians, 43.

BENZON, Zorzi, Proveditor, in Campo, 13; in Regno, 22, 34.
BULGARIANS, 23, 83.

CATASTICATORI, 24, 85.
CORNARO, Girolamo. Letters from Ivanovich, 6, 55, 100. Rival of Morosini, 48, 49, 51, 52. Fails at Santa Maura, 48, 94. In Dalmatia, 49, 94. Takes Castel Nuovo, 49, 95. Honors, 50. Asks reinforcements, 51. Takes Knin, 52, 98. Elected Captain General, 93.

DARDUINO, Lauro, 19, 80.
DOLFIN, Daniel, Quarto, Proveditor Straordinario in Campo, 11, 12, 41, 42, 84.

EMO, Giorgio, Commissario Pagatore, 24, 86.

GALOPPO, Girolamo, 84.
GIUSTINIANO, Marc Antonio, Doge, 24, 25, 86-87.

HOMBERGK, Ulrich Friedrich, Hessian Ensign, 92.

IVANOVICH, Cristoforo. His *Istoria della Lega Ortodossa*, 3, 7, 59, 65. Life, 3-5, 60-64. Writings, 4-6, 59, 60, 62. Letters to Cornaro and Morosini, 6, 54, 55, 100. Tomb, 6, 64. Death and Will, 7, 65. Arms, 60.

KÖNIGSMARK, Otto Wilhelm von, 10, 11, 53, 71.

LA RUE, Rinaldo de, 45, 70.

MEGARA. Abandoned and burned, 15, 18, 76. Description, 17-18, 77-78.
MISTRA. Quarantined because of plague, 15, 21, 33. Description and history, 16, 77. Given to Mainiotes, 21. Fate of inhabitants, 21-22, 34-36, 89-90. Offers to surrender, 20, 32, 76. Terms of surrender, 33.
MOROSINI, Francesco, Captain General, Doge. Reluctant to attack Athens, 3, 66. Letters from Ivanovich, 6, 55, 100. Welcomed by Athenians, 10. Orders bombardment of Parthenon(?), 10, 69. Receives surrender of Turks, 12. Visits Athens, 12, 71.

Terror caused by his success, 15. Orders burning of Megara, 15, 18, 76. Reports capture of Athens to Senate, 18, 78. Decides to abandon Athens, 20, 37-39, 91. Later ill-fortune, 20, 36, 80. Visits Nauplia, 21, 81. Treatment of Mistriotes, 21, 22, 35-36, 89. Gathers army at Poros, 23. Elected Doge, 25, 87, 93. Criticism of election, 26, 47-48. Rivalry with Cornaro, 48, 51, 97. Captures Santa Maura, 48. Resents diversion of allied troops, 49, 94. Offers to resign, 50, 95, 96. Asks reinforcements against Negroponte, 52, 82. Relations with German officers and Königsmark, 53, 92, 99. Grounds of opposition to him, 53, 54, 98. Confidence of Senate, 54. His character according to Garzoni, 54. Raid on Piraeus in 1654, 67.

MOROSINI, Pietro, nephew of Francesco, 21, 99.
MUTONI, Antonio, Conte di San Felice, 10, 11, 13, 70, 72-73.

NAPOLI DI MALVASIA (Monemvasia), 9, 21, 23, 32, 34, 35.
NAPOLI DI ROMANIA (Nauplia), 21, 30, 81, 83.
NEGROPONTE, 23, 31, 46, 52, 53, 71, 80, 82, 84-85, 91, 92, 94, 97, 99, 100.

PARTHENON, 10, 11, 13, 14, 69-70, 73.
PLAGUE. In Mistra, 15, 33. In the Morea, 37, 38. In Athens and the army, 37, 40-46. In Thebes, 40. Reports sent to Venice, 44, 45-46.
POMPEI, Conte Tomeo, 13.
PORTO LIONE. Description, 9, 68. Fortified by wall and trench, 39. Raided in 1654, 67.
PORTO PORO (Poros), 23, 43, 45, 46.

RANUCCIO II Farnese, Duke of Parma, 24, 60, 86.

SAN FELICE, Conte di, see MUTONI.
STORMS during winter, 19, 79.

TURENNE, Louis, Prince de, 12, 29-31.
TURKS. Defend Acropolis, 10-12. Leave for Smyrna, 12, 72. Plan campaign in 1688, 23, 81-83. Fortify Negroponte, 23, 84. Attempt raids in Attica, 75-76.

VENETIAN, ARMY. Leaves Corinth, 9. Strength on landing at Piraeus, 9, 67. Losses during siege, 15, 75; from plague, 43-46. Winter quarters in Athens, 19, 75, 79. Builds four redoubts, 75. Withdrawal to Poros, 22, 23, 43, 92.
    FLEET, 19, 79.
    OFFICERS. At siege of Acropolis, 13, 72. In danger of drowning, 21, 80-81.
VENIER, Lorenzo, Capitan Straordinario delle Navi, 21, 79, 80, 83.

Augsburg College
George Sverdrup Library
Minneapolis, Minnesota 55404

WITHDRAWN